My Love Letters to The Grieving

You Are Not Alone

30-Day Devotional of Companionship, Guidance & God's Comfort Toward Healing

Ke'Shawn Hill-Adamson

www.TrueVinePublishing.org

My Love Letters to the Grieving
Ke'Shawn Hill-Adamson

Published by True Vine Publishing Co
810 Dominican Dr.
Nashville, TN 37228
www.TrueVinePublishing.org

ISBN: 978-1-968092-29-0 Paperback
ISBN:978-1-968092-28-3 eBook

Dedications

I dedicate my first book to my Lord and Savior, Jesus Christ. May You be glorified through every story and every tear, and may it add a harvest to Your Kingdom. Only You could have birthed this masterpiece. Thank You for entrusting me with Your precious souls and with this sacred work.

The King of my heart, I love You forever and ever, Abba Father, and always.

First, honoring my Mommy, and my family, Kim, and Prince Jr. This work is for us, and it's just the beginning. May our family's legacy, and the legacy of those who have gone home before us, never die. Let every day we live, we recover, rebound, heal, and find our greatest purpose in our pain from all our losses.

Let "Mommy," "Daddy," Drew, Prince III, and all our family get to live through us. The Lord's promise to us, to our bloodline, to Heal Our Land:

Isaiah 61 (NIV)

1 The Spirit of the Sovereign Lord is on me, because The Lord has anointed me to proclaim good news to the poor. He has sent me to bind up the brokenhearted, to proclaim freedom for the captives and release from darkness for the prisoners,
2 to proclaim the year of The Lord's favor and the day of vengeance of our God, to comfort all who mourn,
3 and provide for those who grieve in Zion, to bestow on

them a crown of beauty instead of ashes, the oil of joy instead of mourning, and a garment of praise instead of a spirit of despair. They will be called oaks of righteousness, a planting of The Lord for the display of his splendor.

4 They will rebuild the ancient ruins and restore the places long devastated; they will renew the ruined cities that have been devastated for generations.

5 Strangers will shepherd your flocks; foreigners will work your fields and vineyards.

6 And you will be called priests of The Lord, you will be named ministers of our God. You will feed on the wealth of nations, and in their riches you will boast.

7 Instead of your shame you will receive a double portion, and instead of disgrace you will rejoice in your inheritance. And so you will inherit a double portion in your land, and everlasting joy will be yours.

8 "For I, The Lord, love justice; I hate robbery and wrongdoing. In my faithfulness I will reward my people and make an everlasting covenant with them.

9 Their descendants will be known among the nations and their offspring among the peoples. All who see them will acknowledge that they are a people The Lord has blessed."

10 I delight greatly in The Lord; my soul rejoices in my God. For he has clothed me with garments of salvation and arrayed me in a robe of his righteousness, as a bridegroom adorns his head like a priest, and as a bride adorns herself with her jewels.

11 For as the soil makes the sprout come up and a garden causes seeds to grow, so the Sovereign Lord will

make righteousness and praise spring up before all nations.

To my mother, Pamela Patterson, my angel, the wind beneath my wings. Thank you for being my rock, my constant, my everything all my life. Thank you for fighting for me and Kim, for your family, and for the call of God through all our heartbreak and losses. I watched your evolution through motherhood, through major losses, and with Christ. You have stayed the course, kept your eyes on Christ, and kept your hand to the plow. "Mommy," "Daddy," Grandpa, and our family would be so proud.

You planted this seed in me when I was a little girl, hopeless and helpless under the weight of grief, and you gave me the gift of prayer. You told me that if I would pray, my prayers could help save someone's life, and it was that day the gift of intercession was born. That one moment changed my life and planted the seed for this book as a pre-teen.

A great woman of God, full of valor, strength, wisdom, honor, dignity, and class; full of humor, light, laughter, kindness, and love. In your meekness, your boldness for your faith is awe-inspiring. You are one of the strongest women I know. You are what resiliency looks like. In your greatest weakness, you have been made strong.

I am who I am because of you. Thank you for every sacrifice. I love you, Mommy, forever and ever.

To my big sister, Kim Wilson-Whynn,
You left behind big shoes to fill growing up. Small

in stature, but a giant in my eyes. You are one of the fly-est girls I've known, everyone's favorite, the brightest star, full of smarts, beauty, determination, and resilience.

I've watched you do hard things first, trailing a path for me to follow. You have absolutely looked after me all my life, no matter where life had taken you, you always looked out for me and came back for me. Between you and Mommy, you stabilized me my entire life.

You were my tribe and village when things were tough, and you looked after me in ways only a big sister could. You have taught me so much. Thank you. Even when we fought like cats and dogs, like siblings do, and sometimes through hurts and pains, we have a lifetime of love and memories.

You are one of my greatest heroes and inspirations, my first best friend. No friend could ever take your spot. Eternally, thank you, for being constant when I needed you the most growing up. I am who I am because of you too. I love you, big Sis!!!

To your Dad, our Dad, Paul, thank you for loving and caring for me like your very own all my life.

To my Uncle, Prince Cureton Jr., You are my ride-or-die, my partner in crime, my brother, and my first buddy. We could laugh for days. We have memories for a lifetime.

On the real, there are no words I could ever say to soothe your soul, comfort your heart, or take away any pain you've endured with the loss of "Mommy," "Daddy," and now your baby boy, your oldest son, Prince Shaquan Cureton III.

Unc, while writing this book, I had you in mind. My

heart was broken with yours, so when you read this, my heart is speaking directly to you. I love you, my fam!!!

Let's make P's life and legacy, "Mommy" and "Daddy's" legacy, be remembered. Let it begin here with us, let this gift be the start. This book is a gift from God to all of us.

I love you, Prince Jr.! For the words I don't get to say, hear them now, and I pray it waters the garden of your heart and produces a harvest.

To my family that have gone home to The Lord, "Mommy," Minnie Ruth Cureton; "Daddy," Prince Cureton Sr.; Grandpa, Dudley Andrew Hill Sr.; Uncle "Drew," Dudley Andrew Hill Jr.; my lil cuz, Prince Shaquan Cureton III; Uncle Danny; Aunt Gloria; Aunt Patsy; Uncle Clifford; Aunt Ora; Cousin Kedrick; Aunt Viviene Thompson; Uncle Jack; Tommy; Great Grandma Fannie; Great Grandma Ida; Mr. Wilson; Grandma Johnnie O'Faire; Brother Olandis "Lammie": Uncle Ray; Uncle Joe; Uncle Larry; Uncle David; Cousin Lavern Hill; college buddy, Andre Fraser; Uncle Ricky; Uncle Howard; Ma Bunny, Mr. Taylor, "Grandma" Abrahams, and so many more.

To my second Dad, Samuel "Pete" Patterson, that raised me, I miss you terribly. We had a rough start growing up, but I glorify God for how He transformed you, me, our relationship, and made it whole. You were my ride-or-die, my safe place, my comforter. You were a wild, crazy teenager with a heart of gold, always ready to give anyone the shirt off your back. I watched you evolve with your walk with God and marveled at what you were becoming, but when God was ready, He called you home.

You shared all of my first moments and became my buddy and best friend. There are no words to describe how much I miss you and how much our lives have changed without you. Your legacy will always live on in me and our family.

I love and miss you, Pete!

To all my family who have gone on, I miss you all so much. Not a day goes by that I'm not thinking about you. Until we meet again, it's not goodbye; it's "I'll see you later."

I love you and I miss you dearly.

This is for you!

With love,
Ke'Shawn

Table of Contents

Foreword

"And ye shall know the truth, and the truth shall make you free" (John 8:32, KJV).

In this world of controversy and deeply rooted opinions, there are few things that everyone can agree on. However, I think almost everyone agrees that losing someone we love is heartbreaking and life-changing. If you have never experienced death, you may not understand the impact of loss. But if you have, especially the death of someone you love, it solidifies two things: first, you are never ready, even when the death has been anticipated and you know it is coming; and second, it is an experience for which there is no clear set of rules, no real guidance, and little preparation.

Ke'Shawn Hill-Adamson has tapped into this raw and uncharted territory in this book. Before you read it, make a commitment to be vulnerable, to allow yourself to enter this experience boldly and without hesitation. It will probably be the first time in your life that you have been asked to experience and express your feelings about death in this way. Because of our socialization and upbringing, most of us have been taught to avoid any discussion of death and to move quickly through the process of grieving when loss occurs. But this book will help you understand the power of confronting grief, expressing grief, and healing from grief so that it does not become the root of physical, psychological, or emotional dysfunction in your life.

Ke'Shawn's honesty and her willingness to expose her own story has given her freedom that she could not have imagined before. Her journey to recover began with her recognition of some very important truths about her life. If we are willing to follow her example, we too can know the truth, and the truth will make us free.

I pray that you find your truth as you journey through these pages. Take advantage of the resources that are provided in the book. Use them for yourself, or to help someone else who is struggling through the journey of grieving. I pray that "the eyes of your understanding will be enlightened" so that you can minister hope to someone who is grieving, especially if they don't even know it.

This book reminds us that although grief is a painful journey, it is not a journey that we must take alone. God is always present with us, even in the painful places, and He has given wisdom to some like Ke'Shawn who can teach us how to triumph over grief and despair. I was tremendously blessed as I read this book, and I believe you will be too.

Rev. Dr. Tresmaine R. Grimes
Co-Pastor, Living Water Christian Center
September 2025

What Others Are Saying About Me

I'm honored to share the kind words of mentors, colleagues, organizations, and those who have hired me along this journey. Their support has been part of God's grace in helping me serve others through grief. These reflections were shared as recommendations about my work and calling. They are not endorsements of this book.

"I personally taught and certified Ke'Shawn as a Grief Educator...She is a Moderator in my Tender Hearts Program, co-leading grief groups for specific losses, and is featured in testimonials on our Grief Educators and Facebook Live commercials...She's articulate and compassionate in her work...I highly recommend her in any capacity in our field. It is truly a pleasure seeing how she continues to be a gift to the world..."

—David Kessler
World-Renowned Grief Expert
Founder of Grief.com

"Ke'Shawn Hill-Adamson completed my public speaking training, 'Own the Power of Your Story,' in the spring of 2022. I witnessed her determination to learn to powerfully share her grief journey so that she could deeply serve others in grief. I'm delighted that she's out there using her voice and making an impact."

—Rachel Hanfling,
Emmy-nominated TV Producer (Oprah & Anderson Cooper)
Media & Communications Trainer
International Keynote Speaker

"I was amazed at how she was able to keep such a large group of students engaged virtually... learning strategies on how to decompress and relieve stress. Her public speaking abilities were one of her strengths..."

—Bloomfield College of Montclair State University, EOF Program

"Ke'Shawn is an empowering guide who embodies compassion, strength, and deep care. Her work in helping people move through grief and loss provides hope for those dealing with deep loss. She is a powerful Grief Movement Guide that I highly recommend."

—Paul Denniston
Founder – Grief Movement Training

"Ke'Shawn is a passionate leader... a woman of excellence... defines integrity. I have had the opportunity to collaborate with Ke'Shawn on developing grief support services for the loss of a loved one... this was an invaluable experience. As a college instructor and employed as the CEO for Hospice, I have been honored to have curated professional relationships with Ke'Shawn and personally endorse her..."

—Demetress Harrell,
CEO, Hospice of The Pines

"Ke'Shawn excels as a Certified Grief Coach and Educator. Ke'Shawn spoke at several events and made a difference on college campuses. Her impact through coaching and public speaking is powerful."

—Ashley Gooden-Stewart,
Founder of Baby Stewart Foundation

"The exercise demonstration was phenomenal. I particularly enjoyed the education on meridian tapping and movements... being mindful about the mental aspect of moving when it comes to emotional processing. This was powerful. I love how Ke'Shawn models how to talk to yourself peacefully and with kindness."

**—Passaic County Community College, Director of Wellness,
Professional Development Series**

Introduction

This book, *My Love Letters to the Grieving: You Are Not Alone – Companionship, Guidance & God's Comfort Toward Healing*, is deeply personal to me. It is the culmination of decades of deep, hidden grief, beginning at the age of seven after losing my beloved grandmother (whom we all affectionately called "Mommy"); decades of cumulative losses; the loss of my second dad, Pete, who helped raise me; and our most recent loss on June 16, 2025, my lil' cousin, Prince Shaquan Cureton III.

This book is the journey of a broken heart and a shattered soul through the many terrains of grief. It's the ugly truths, the despondency, and the despair of grief. It's woven with hard truths, lessons learned, wisdom I've been taught, and the education I've received.

It is the story of how God miraculously resuscitated and breathed life into me time after time after traumatic losses. It is the story of how the Lord's supernatural visitations of His presence comforted me. These moments were coupled with insights on how to allow His love and Word to heal me. It includes practical daily practices that can help us in the moment. It is the story of how, in grief's ugliest moments, God manifested Himself in my deepest pain.

This book is not a quick fix. It's not here to slap a scripture or Band-Aid on your pain. It's not here to bright-side you as if your pain doesn't matter. But in this journey, and in a grief-illiterate world, it offers a fresh look at grief. It normalizes it, giving it a new perspective, and a glimmer of hope in the Word of God.

Grief can feel like the darkest and loneliest place on earth. It's an unbearable pain unlike any other. I lived it, and I've been crafting these stories for years. I watched my uncle lose his oldest son. I saw my friends lose their parents. I lost my second Dad, Pete, and endured the cumulative losses in my life. I also listened to countless stories while moderating specific loss groups for David Kessler's Tender Hearts grief support community. Through all of this, I have seen grief from multiple vantage points.

I've walked these dark, lonely roads. I've been on the sidelines watching the agony, wanting to take each person's pain away, heartbroken because I couldn't. I've learned something life-changing and profound working with David Kessler's team: People don't need to be "fixed." It is not my job to "fix" them. I am incapable of taking their pain away. There are no words in the human language that could possibly take away their pain.

The best thing I can do is sit with them and meet them where they are, to accept them where they are, whatever that looks like. So with this book, it's a place where we sit together. It's a place to be seen. A place to be heard, affirmed and validated. It's a place where there is no shame, and a place where you don't have to make excuses for where you are on your journey.

Here, we simply sit. We learn. We ponder. We reflect. We cry. We laugh. We feel. We process, and we give ourselves permission to grieve.

I watched the people I love suffer under the weight of grief. I saw the depth of their despair. In my small way, if God can use my pain and turn it into something that breathes life, gives guidance, and offers support in someone's darkest hour, that is redemption for me.

There is no death I would want to sacrifice. There is no price I would want to pay to see the greatest good come from it. I have endured much under the weight of death. But if my pain could serve others in their healing, that would be healing for me too.

If it could breathe life, offer light, give hope, and guide the brokenhearted to recover, it would still not bring my family back. It would not take my pain away. But somehow, some way, that is redemption for me, and their deaths will not be in vain.

My one prayer for my life to The Lord is: Heal my land. It's my very prayer for you too!

So, in this deep, dark place, I want you to know: You are not alone. You are deeply seen. You are deeply loved. What you are going through matters. We sit and grieve together. You matter. Your story matters. How your loved one died matters. What you feel matters. Your loved one's life and Legacy, their fingerprint, and the impact they had on the earth long after they are gone, matter!

Your life, your purpose, and your unique fingerprint on the earth, despite your loss, STILL MATTER! I created this work so that, on those lonely days, you can feel you are not alone. You are seen, held, accepted as you are. You are guided, comforted, and loved right where you stand. It is my prayer that God will reveal Himself to you in a new way, that you would feel a deeper love, a fresh awareness of His presence, and that you would find a spark of hope.

Sometimes, it won't happen instantly. Healing takes time, but in this space where we sit and commune together with God, it is my prayer something miraculous can occur that will help you hold on. For our moments together, God's presence can cause a shift to occur. Through space and time, out of your tragedy, one millisecond at a time, He can give you beauty for your ashes, or at the very least, comfort for the moment.

From my heart to yours, I love you. I'm thinking of you. You are on my mind today, and I am praying for you through your process. These are my love letters to you. Receive them with love.

In your deepest hour, may God pour out His Spirit, His power, His presence, and His rest, and may He give you peace. In Jesus' mighty name, Amen!

I love you, and I'm thinking about you.

With love,
Ke'Shawn

Your Pain Matters

*I*f I say nothing else to you today, please know this: your pain matters. Your pain is seen. You are seen, and what you're going through matters. There are no words in the human dictionary that could ever fully console, comfort, or bring you healing. Nothing I could say would take away the pain, the despondency, the agony, or magically make it better.

I can't fully relate to your loss by bringing up my losses in an effort to comfort you, because the truth is every loss is different. Your loved one was different. Your loss is different. Your pain is exclusively yours.

I stand here helpless, wanting to take away the hurt. But the best thing I can do is simply sit with you to let you know: your pain matters. You matter. The life of your loved one, and even the way they died, matters.

I'm so sorry for your loss. I'm sorry you are here. I'm sorry we met this way. I'm sorry we both sit here helpless together. And yet, even in this moment, I'm grateful. Grateful to share this space with you. Sometimes in grief, just having your pain seen and acknowledged is enough.

We often feel helpless watching those we love agonize over their loss. In those moments, what's needed most isn't words that try to fix the pain; it's presence. It's in the quiet that we truly acknowledge pain, where we simply sit with it, and with each other.

So today, I sit with you. I know I can't fix this for you. But I can be with you, acknowledge your pain, and share in it. Today, if nothing else, I want you to hold onto this truth: You are seen. If no one else gets it, in this moment, I get it. Most importantly, God gets it. You matter. Your pain matters.

I love you and I'm thinking about you.

With love,
Ke'Shawn

SRIPTURE

"When Jesus saw her weeping, and the Jews who had come along with her also weeping, he was deeply moved in spirit and troubled. "'Where have you laid him?' he asked. Jesus wept" (**John 11:33–35, NIV**).

"She gave this name to The Lord who spoke to her: 'You are the God who sees me,' for she said, 'I have now seen the One who sees me'" (**Genesis 16:13, NIV**).

"When they saw him from a distance, they could hardly recognize him; they began to weep aloud, and they tore their robes and sprinkled dust on their heads. Then they sat on the ground with him for seven days and seven nights. No one said a word to him, because they saw how great his suffering was" (**Job 2:12–13, NIV**).

REFLECTION

Even the Savior of the world felt deep empathy and compassion as He watched the people around Him grieving. He was moved. He was troubled. He understood. Jesus wept over the pain and loss that touches every one of us. Death was never God's intention; it was always for life. So, He weeps knowing the pain and destruction it causes and how it breaks the hearts of His people.

The Son of God wept, and He's weeping with you right now. He feels everything you are feeling. He knows the depths of your pain. In the scripture with Job, his friends sat with him for seven days and said nothing; they simply sat with him in his distress. They had that part right in the beginning. What I never understood is that the concept of sitting with someone in quiet in their grief is very biblical. There's something holy, sacred, and healing about sitting with someone in the quiet.

Is it uncomfortable? Yes! Even for me. But I'm learning to allow the stillness to speak, to allow the moment and God to provide the healing in the stillness. Our minds tell us we have to be doing something to make everything better, but the truth is, that's a knee-jerk reaction coming from our minds, not our hearts. Without even knowing it, you're helping someone else heal while you sit and grieve with them.

The Lord sits and grieves with you too. There's healing available as you simply sit in God's presence and allow Jesus to tend to your wounds. Here's a promise: He will not leave you alone. You may feel isolated and lonely, but you are not alone. The Lord is right here with you, weeping alongside you, comforting you, and fully understanding your pain. You are seen by God. He cares. He is with you.

I love you, and I'm thinking of you.

With love,
Ke'Shawn

REFLECTION QUESTIONS

1. In what ways do you need to be truly seen right now?
2. What do you wish others better understood about your grief?
3. What support or comfort do you need right now to help you through your process?

PRAYER

Father, in the name of Jesus, I thank You that You see me. You don't just look down and watch me; you know me intimately. You know my coming and my going. You know my thoughts. You know when I lie down and when I rise up.

You know the number of hairs on my head. You created me in the innermost parts of my mother's womb. Father, I feel so unseen right now. People just don't get it; they couldn't get it. Lord, I know You see what I'm going through right now. Sometimes, I feel like You're far away, but today, by faith, I ask You to increase my faith and remove every doubt that You're distant from my pain.

Despite how I feel, I'm choosing to believe You are walking beside me. Miraculously reveal Yourself to me; let me feel You. Comfort me while I'm sleeping. When I feel faint and can walk no longer, I believe You are carrying me. Carry me now, Lord, because I need You.

I love You, and I thank You for hearing and answering my prayer.

In Jesus' mighty name, Amen.

DAY 1
JOURNAL

_____

_____

_____

_____

_____

_____

_____

_____

_____

_____

_____

_____

_____

_____

_____

_____

_____

_____

_____

_____

_____

Even If...

*A*fter loss, it's almost impossible not to look back and wonder what we could have done differently. For me, after every loss, my mind replayed those questions: Did I do enough? Did they know how much I loved them? Could I have changed the outcome?

I should have said... I wish I would've called. If I had done that, maybe they wouldn't have died.

Should've, could've, would've replay in our minds. As if grief itself weren't already enough to carry, the torment of guilt makes it unbearable. This is called the **"what if"** stage, also known as **bargaining**, where we replay scenarios in our minds, wishing we could change the outcome. When I was just a little girl and my grandmother passed away, I remember feeling responsible. I thought, "Maybe if I hadn't driven her crazy by jumping on her bed the night before, she wouldn't have gotten sick and died."

That's a heavy burden for a child to carry. It didn't stop there. Over the years, after every death, I've wondered: Did I do the right thing? If I had said or done something different, would it have changed anything?

"I didn't get a chance to say goodbye." Sometimes, it's not only the pain of loss that breaks you, it's the guilt and shame that won't let you go. You might be wrestling right now with that same thought: If only I had done this..., If only I had said that..., because of what I did or didn't do, they might still be alive. David Kessler has always taught us: "Our minds would always rather feel guilty than helpless. In grief, guilt can feel like control. It gives us something to hold onto, even if it hurts. Feeling helpless is sometimes unbearable."

Grief makes you feel vulnerable and helpless, and those feelings alone can make you angry. No one likes to feel out of control, especially when it comes to protecting the people we love. It's built into us to want to save them, and when something happens, we naturally believe we could have fixed it.

But here's the hardest truth: hindsight is 20/20. You don't know what you don't know. Sometimes, no matter how hard we try or what decisions we make, we can't always protect the ones we love.

We're not strong enough. We're not wise enough. We're not all-knowing or all-powerful enough. We're not everywhere at all times. Only God is!

If it were truly in our control to alter the lives of those we love, to protect them, we absolutely, hands down, would have. But when we take that burden on ourselves, we step into a role that only belongs to God. We carry guilt and shame that were never meant for our shoulders. That type of weight eats you alive. Guilt is like a cancer. It erodes you from the inside and slowly kills your spirit, soul, body, and your future.

So today, I invite you to do something different: Replace the words "If only I..." with "Even if I had." Even if you had done this or that differently, it still may not have changed the outcome. I don't know your circumstance, and I don't know the details of your loved one's death, but here's what I do know: we are not in control of the birth date or transition date of our loved ones. God only knows our beginning from our end.

So, I say this with so much love and as gently as I can. I do not say it to explain away your pain or to bright -side you. I say it because I feel led to share it and because of what I have learned in my training. Even if you had done xyz, the truth is that we cannot control all things. Even if you had done everything right, they still may have died.

I know, I know, I may not get what you feel right now, no one may. You may feel 100% responsible and releasing that may take God's truth and a whole lot of time. No one understands how you feel, the regrets you may have, or the lies the enemy tells to make you feel responsible or guilty.

But here's what I hear The Lord saying to you right now: "Give it to Me! That burden you carry, release it to Me. I AM the Alpha and Omega, the beginning and the end. I AM your burden bearer and desire to lift the guilt and shame off your neck. Whatever it is, I forgive you, I'm not mad at you, and I love you with my everything, and I release you to forgive yourself, whatever you are carrying.

Whisper to Me, 'Father, I feel _____ about _____, and I give You my regret of _____. You love and forgive me, so I will love, forgive, and release myself of _____ and give it to You right now in Jesus' name.'"

It takes time to believe this, but you are human. Keep repeating that prayer in faith. Here's the truth: You have limited capacity, limited power, limited control, and if you could have done something different, if you had truly known, you absolutely would have. Yes, sometimes we play a part in how things turn out, but we don't know what we don't know. We are flawed human beings without perfect vision, without foresight, without the ability to change every outcome.

My prayer for you today is this: That you supernaturally receive a deep knowing that you are only human. That you feel it in your bones; it's not your fault. You couldn't predict the future. You didn't have the power to alter someone else's destiny. I pray The Lord's Spirit releases upon you power to:

- Show compassion for yourself.
- Take yourself off the hook.
- Forgive yourself.
- Receive revelation that you are frail and human, just like every one of us.
- Recognize that you are without power or control over anyone's fate.

So today, replace the "If only" with "Even if" and let God be God. I'm praying deep peace and comfort over you, that the truth will wash over your heart, that guilt and shame will lift off you, and that you will finally be able to forgive yourself.

I love you, and I'm thinking about you.

With love,
Ke'Shawn

SCRIPTURE

"Show me, LORD, my life's end and the number of my days; let me know how fleeting my life is. You have made my days a mere handbreadth; the span of my years is as nothing before you. Everyone is but a breath, even those who seem secure" **(Psalm 39:4–5, NIV).**

REFLECTION

God alone numbers our days. It's not you. It's not me. It's not anyone else who determines the moment we are born or the moment we leave this life.

Only He knows the beginning from the end. We are merely vessels passing through this earth, and the truth is only God is fully in control. At our best efforts, He is still sovereign, sits on His throne, and orchestrates the affairs of our lives.

I pray you find rest and peace in His sovereignty, knowing that every moment of your life and every moment of your loved one's life has always been safely held in His hands.

REFLECTION QUESTIONS

1. What do you need to make peace with today?
2. What are you wrestling with or feeling guilty about?
3. How can you turn "If only" into "Even if" and release that burden to God?
4. How can you take comfort in what you did right by your loved one?

PRAYER

Father, in the name of Jesus, I come to You weighed down with guilt. Thoughts of what I should have done, could have done, would have done torment my mind. Touch my mind right now. Touch my heart that won't release this guilt.

You said there is no condemnation for those in Christ Jesus, and that the enemy comes only to kill, steal, and destroy. So, Father, pull down every thought, every imagination, every lie hijacking my mind that the enemy is using to torment me. Release to me the mind of Christ to think on what is true, right, noble, pure, lovely, excellent, and praiseworthy.

I thank You for supernaturally transforming my mind to think how You think, to see how You see, to hear how You hear, and I thank You for silencing every force of darkness that tries to keep me trapped in guilt.

Reveal to me the gift of Your forgiveness towards me and grace to help me forgive myself. Remind me of all the ways and things I've done to honor my loved one and allow gratitude to lead me to peace.

In Jesus' mighty name, Amen.

DAY 2
JOURNAL

_____

_____

_____

_____

_____

_____

_____

_____

_____

_____

_____

_____

_____

_____

_____

_____

_____

_____

_____

_____

_____

_____

Giving Your Pain A Voice

I love the movie *Inside Out*. It's a Disney Pixar film created to help children identify their emotions. I often use that movie as an example, even when I'm coaching adults, because in its simplest, most childlike way, it reminds us that it's okay to feel.

Somewhere in my adulting, I forgot that.

As children, we're supposed to learn how to name and express our feelings. But somewhere along the way, many of us were taught that emotions weren't safe. That feelings made others uncomfortable. That to "be okay," we had to shove them down, push them out, and silence what was truly happening inside.

That's why I love Robert Plutchik's work on the **Wheel of Emotions.** In 1980, he created this model to show how complex and interconnected our emotions really are. It helps us identify and name the feelings we experience, especially when they're tangled and overwhelming.

And grief? Grief has a way of silencing us. In my grief, I learned how to pretend I was "okay," how to keep smiling while hiding the storm inside. But that wasn't okay. I wasn't okay. Over time, all those unspoken feelings catch up with you.

Grief is like a string of Christmas lights hopelessly tangled in a box. You try to unravel the wires, to make sense of it all, but the knots only tighten in your hands.

Grief can bring on multiple emotions all at once. One moment you may feel sadness, the next rage, then disbelief. Sometimes you feel all of them at the same time, spinning in every direction with no off switch.

There's no minimum or maximum to how long these feelings will last. Emotions in grief don't follow rules. They come in waves, they overlap, and sometimes, as long as you're grieving, they stay with you.

For many of us, anger feels the strongest. You might be angry that your loved one died.

Angry about the circumstances surrounding their death.

Angry at people who showed up, or those who didn't. Angry at what people said, or what they didn't say. Even angry because you stubbed your toe and it felt like one more unbearable thing. Sometimes it feels like you're angry at everything under the sun.

Here's what I've learned: Anger is pain's bodyguard. It's not here to harm you. It's here to shield you from the deep, raw sadness underneath. The worst thing you can do is push those feelings down or pretend they don't exist.

Your feelings have names. They matter. They deserve space and time. They won't go away until they are addressed and processed. Like a child, they want, need, and demand attention.

It's okay to be angry, and you should be. It's okay to be sad, and you should be. It's okay to feel disbelief, and that's normal! What you're thinking and feeling is normal. Show yourself compassion. Allow yourself to feel and release without judgment. Your emotions aren't weaknesses; they're signs that your pain needs to be seen and heard.

You might try journaling what you feel, joining a support group, or talking with a trusted friend. When words fail, when no one else seems to understand, remember this: God is a safe place to land. He never tires of hearing your voice. He never turns away when you wrestle with Him in your tears, in your questions, and in your pain.

With Him, you are safe. Come, give it all to Him.
I love you and I'm thinking about you.

With love,
Ke'Shawn

SCRIPTURE

"A time to weep and a time to laugh, a time to mourn and a time to dance" **(Ecclesiastes 3:4, NIV).**

REFLECTION

There is a season for every emotion under the sun. The Lord invites you to embrace each moment and every feeling, knowing they are all a part of your healing journey. Whatever you're feeling right now, it's okay.

REFLECTION QUESTIONS

1. How are you feeling right now, in this very moment?
2. What emotions are rising up within you? Can you name them?
3. What can you do today to give those feelings a safe place to be heard?

PRAYER

Father, in the name of Jesus, I pray for courage to give my pain a voice. I pray for boldness to confront the things that are too hard to feel. You grant me grace to feel my feelings without shame or apology, and that every moment I come to You, You release in me peace, that You're steady, You're present, You're listening, holding, and comforting me moment by moment.

In Jesus' mighty name, Amen.

DAY 3
JOURNAL

_____
_____
_____
_____
_____
_____
_____
_____
_____
_____
_____
_____
_____
_____
_____
_____
_____
_____
_____
_____
_____
_____
_____

Give Yourself Permission to Grieve

I learned about **Elisabeth Kübler-Ross** in college in my Death and Dying class. She developed the **"Five Stages of Grief"** while working with terminally ill patients to help explain what they were feeling as they faced their own death. Over time, this model has also helped those grieving the loss of someone they love. Understanding these stages of grief helped me better understand my process, and that what I was going through had a name.

The stages include **disbelief, anger, bargaining, depression, and acceptance.** David Kessler later added a sixth stage: finding meaning.

- **Disbelief:** This is the "I can't believe this happened" stage. Everything feels unreal, and your mind may struggle to accept the loss.
- **Anger:** Feeling mad at the situation, at others, at yourself, or even at life itself. Anger often hides deeper pain.
- **Bargaining:** The "what if" stage, where we replay scenarios in our minds, wishing we could change the outcome.
- **Depression:** The deep sadness and heaviness that comes from missing someone and processing the loss.

- **Acceptance:** The stage where you come to terms with the reality of the loss. This doesn't mean you're "okay," but you begin to find a way to live with it.
- **Finding meaning:** Recognizing that even in loss, life has purpose, and there may be lessons, growth, or new understanding that come from your grief.

Real talk: Grief is unbearable. It follows you wherever you go with no break in sight. I know you long for relief. You want a break from the weight of it all, but sometimes it feels like that break never comes. The truth is, this grieving process is unbearably hard. Agonizing.

The reality is we are not in control of our grieving process. We can't rush it or force ourselves to heal. Grief will never magically disappear because it will be our life-long companion as long as we've loved someone deeply. I know what you're already saying: you're over it. I know, and I'm so sorry for the pain you're in. I'm over it too. It's that part of life that's unavoidable, and the part that we hate.

Yet, even though the pain we feel is unbearable, in time, the process can also be truly transformative. If we allow grief to have its way and do its work in us, one day, one millisecond at a time, we slowly move closer toward healing. Don't rush yourself through the process. Healing takes time. It took me decades to understand that the more you rush, pretend you're not grieving, or avoid learning about grief, the longer you prolong the cycle of suffering.

Grief is a lifelong journey. It's not linear. It's not quick, and there's nothing you can do to simply "fix it."

You have to honor where you are in the process and the stages you find yourself in.

Sometimes, the only way out is through. It's okay to grieve. It's okay to be sad. Others may not like your process or feel uncomfortable with your grief, but it's yours. Honor it, because grief is love. You're grieving because you loved and you lost, and that's okay.

Finding meaning and acceptance doesn't happen overnight. It's a process that truly transforms you from the inside out. I know you can't see it now, and while I was in it, I couldn't see it either.

There is truly transformative power in honoring where you are and giving yourself space and permission to grieve. What you avoid will follow you. What you feel will transform you. I couldn't face my grief for decades, but The Lord gave me courage. When I was ready, I did. I believe by faith He will give you the same courage and boldness to walk through any door necessary for your healing, growth, and purpose.

Even if you can't fathom the thought right now, I'm holding onto faith for you. I want you to know, more importantly, The Lord wants you to know, that you are stronger than you realize. I know everything in you feels crushed and weak, but in your weakness, He is valiantly strong within you. He will not let you fall. He's holding you up, and when you are fainting, He's carrying you. He will never let you go!

I love you, and I'm thinking of you.

With love,
Ke'Shawn

SCRIPTURE

"There is a time for everything, and a season for every activity under the heavens: a time to be born and a time to die, a time to plant and a time to uproot, a time to kill and a time to heal, a time to tear down and a time to build, a time to weep and a time to laugh, a time to mourn and a time to dance..." **(Ecclesiastes 3:1–8, NIV).**

REFLECTION

Grief has no timeline. Healing is not a race, and you don't need to meet anyone's expectations about where you "should" be. Whatever you're feeling, it's normal. What you are experiencing is normal. There is no right or wrong to your process. It's yours, and it's okay. God says it's okay. No matter what you're feeling or thinking, He loves and meets you exactly where you are.

This season, whether it feels like disbelief, deep sadness, anger, or numbness, is part of your love story with the one you lost. Give yourself permission to fully experience this part of the journey, knowing that every tear, every pause, and every step is seen and held by God. One day, by faith, this deep, dark season will shift and birth healing in time.

REFLECTION QUESTIONS

1. Can you identify or relate to any stage of grief you're in right now?
2. How do you feel about it?
3. What do you wish could be different right now about where you find yourself in grief?

PRAYER

Father God, in the name of Jesus, sometimes I have to be brutally honest and just say I don't want to come into Your presence because I don't want to feel. I pray for courage and boldness to grieve exactly how I need to grieve, for the fear in me to be eradicated, or perhaps the courage to overcome my fear.

Thank You that You are big enough, loving enough to accept me exactly where I am without judgment or fear.

I thank You for giving me the courage of a lion to stand tall in the midst of my grief and suffering, and I thank You for it.

In Jesus' mighty name, Amen.

DAY 4
JOURNAL

_____
_____
_____
_____
_____
_____
_____
_____
_____
_____
_____
_____
_____
_____
_____
_____
_____
_____
_____
_____
_____
_____
_____
_____

Gratitude

Sometimes in grief, the recurring theme every single day is helplessness. That feeling shows up often: the inability to fix anything, the unending weight you carry after losing someone you love. In those moments, all you can see and feel is pain. There is no joy. There is no peace. There is no place you can run to where it suddenly feels better.

In this space of raw sorrow, I've learned something unexpected: **Gratitude** can be a soft place to land. Gratitude doesn't erase pain. It's not toxic positivity that pretends everything is okay or tries to silence grief. It's not forcing yourself to smile when your heart is shattered.

Instead, gratitude is different. It's the quiet act of digging for treasure in the darkness. It's the faint ember of hope that flickers even in hopelessness. It's saying: Despite my pain, there is still something, no matter how small, I can be thankful for.

So today, just for this moment, let's pause together. Take a deep breath. Set down the weight for just a heartbeat, and let's search gently: What is one thing you can be grateful for right now?

One thing I could be grateful for is that although I lost my dad, Pete, God gave me layers of covering and multiple fathers who have each played and continue to play a significant role in my life, from my grandfather, my biological dad, and Pete. Each played a significant role in my life, reminding me that I was adored and loved, each shaping me in different ways. This is gratitude. Although my grandfather and Pete are no longer alive, my biological dad is still blessed to be with us; being a strong anchor and still making memories. His presence has been, and will always be, everything to me.

I know. You might already be shaking your head, saying, "There's nothing. I can't think of anything." But sometimes gratitude hides in the smallest places. Maybe you can think of something you're grateful for because of your loved one:

- That you got to know them at all.
- That you had the gift of loving and being loved by them.
- That you shared time, even if it feels far too short.
- That you made memories together that now live on forever.
- That their life, their lessons, their presence made you better.

Sometimes, that's all we have when grief feels unbearable. We can't see the forest for the trees. Joy feels far away. Hope feels silent. But even here, especially here, if we dig deep enough, we can find one small, sacred thing to hold on to with gratitude, and sometimes, that's enough to keep going and help get us through tough moments.

I love you and I'm thinking of you.

With love,
Ke'Shawn

SCRIPTURE

"Finally, brothers and sisters, whatever is true, whatever is noble, whatever is right, whatever is pure, whatever is lovely, whatever is admirable—if anything is excellent or praiseworthy—think about such things" **(Philippians 4:8, NIV).**

REFLECTION

I know right now it may feel impossible to find treasure in the darkness. When you find yourself going down into a dark hole, allow gratitude to be a soft place to land. Look for something that can bring you joy, a smile, and reflect on it. Hold onto it tight and allow it to help ground you in this moment.

Gratitude can help stabilize you and focus your heart on what's still important in the midst of your pain.

REFLECTION QUESTIONS

1. What is something you're grateful for at this very moment?
2. How can you allow gratitude to quietly coexist with pain, bringing even a flicker of hope to your heart?

PRAYER

Father God, in the name of Jesus, I thank You for flooding my mind and reminding me of the things that still remain and that I can be grateful for. I pray You give me eyes to see, that I will cherish every moment I remain here on earth, even without my loved one. Help me to know that because I live, I still have meaning and purpose upon the earth, and that they live on in me.

Help me not to lose that focus and to practice gratitude every step of the way. When joy isn't in sight, when gratitude feels faint, remind me and flood my mind with the oil of Your joy. Allow Your presence to overwhelm me and bring me back to life again.

You are my only joy, the hope and light of my heart. Resuscitate me again and again, and let Your love overshadow me when I'm at my weakest.

In Jesus' mighty name, Amen.

DAY 5
JOURNAL

A Gentle Anchor in the Midst of the Storm

Some losses shake us to our very core because how someone dies truly matters. We all grieve when we lose someone we love. When that loss comes through violence, tragedy, immense suffering, trauma, or abruptly, it can feel like it shatters your soul, taking your last breath away. There are no words for the pain of loving someone deeply and then watching their life end in such a heartbreaking way. This kind of grief is indescribable.

Even as I write to you now, I feel speechless. There is nothing I could possibly say that would remove the agony, the torment, or the unbearable weight you may be feeling in this moment. My heart aches with you. I am so, so sorry. All I can do right now is sit with you in spirit and allow The Lord to speak through me, hoping His words reach your heart. Please don't be offended by my attempts; they come from love.

I want you to know, I am so deeply sorry. Death is never easy. Loss is never easy, and when that loss is tragic, my heart is especially with you today. When a loved one's death is violent or traumatic, our minds can get caught in a painful loop, replaying the moment again and again. It can feel like you can't escape, as though you're trapped in that moment with them, unable to break free.

Here's what I've learned: healing this part of grief takes time. It will not happen overnight. But with gentle practice, there are ways to quiet those tormenting memories so they no longer consume you. These practices won't take away the pain, but in a moment of crisis, they can help calm your nervous system, regulate your mind, and help you dig your feet into your faith with the hope of bringing you comfort. Again, this is not a quick fix, but a lifeline in a moment when your mind, body, and soul are unraveling, to ground you.

In my grief work, I don't mix my religion or faith in my practice. However, as I've been taught, understanding what your **belief systems** are (what your faith says about life, death, and what comes after) can bring immense comfort, peace, and calm to the storm you might be facing. It's not a quick fix or a Band-Aid to say, "Oh, my loved one is in heaven, I should rejoice!" or "They're no longer in pain," as if that takes away the pain or lessens the grief we're struggling with because they're no longer with us.

Understanding your belief system can help ground you. It stabilizes you when the grief, thoughts, and emotions are more than you can handle. It also brings you a sense of comfort.

1. UNDERSTANDING WHAT YOUR FAITH SAYS ABOUT LIFE AFTER DEATH

When tragedy happens, it's normal to feel angry at God. We're taught that it's not okay to ask why or to be angry at God. I'm here to tell you, that's the furthest thing from the truth. What we think or feel is okay. It's normal to want to know why something happened and to ask God why, and it's okay to be angry at Him too. He can handle our questions and anger. After all, He's the King over the universe.

Even if you feel doubt or anger toward God right now, it's okay. He understands your pain and your questions. He can handle your anger and pain, and it's okay to let Him know. He wants to hear it.

He wants to really hear how you really feel. Do we need to honor Him? Absolutely. But in this place with Him, you get to keep it real and be who you are with Him. After all, He made you. If in your anger, you sin, you can ask for forgiveness and He will pardon you. He gets you!

After our loved ones die, we may feel an array of things: anger, disappointment at God, or frustrations. Sometimes we feel let down, asking why He allowed these types of tragedies to happen. That too is okay. When these things happen, they really do challenge our faith and shake what we believe. After a traumatic loss, it can either strengthen your faith, shake it, or break it.

It is the enemy's number one goal to separate you from The Lord, so in this moment, it's important to establish what you believe. If your belief is broken, like Jacob, it's okay to wrestle with God too, with your anger and questions. Will this process happen overnight? Absolutely not. This will be a lifelong process, and for some, your faith may waver.

As I've said before, we can't slap a Scripture on our pain and think it will get better. But as we spend time with God, pray for revelation, and courage to face our pain, The Lord can reveal Himself to you and quiet the storm within you. Pray to the Holy Spirit to guide you in spirit and in truth.

I know sitting in silence in His presence may be extremely hard for some; for me, that part was unbearable. But one day, He gave me courage. I believe He'll give you courage too, to face whatever is needed for your healing.

One moment in time, His Word began to calm my storms unlike anything else. I could sense His comfort, and in this place, I could begin to feel the pain and release it little by little. This took time, decades, but He began to heal me. He is no respecter of persons. If He did it for me, He'll do it for you.

As you sojourn through this valley, as you work on your faith, let what you believe gently anchor your loved one in truth. Ask yourself:

- What do I believe about life after death?
- What does my faith or belief system say about where my loved one is now?
- Are they at peace?
- Are they reliving that painful moment, or have they been set free from it forever?

If you believe they are in heaven, or you believe they are asleep, remind your soul that they are no longer suffering, even if your mind keeps replaying their final moments. This will take time. Sometimes you'll need support from professionals to help you process this. But the more you anchor yourself in Scripture and remind yourself of what you believe, the more it can help quiet the storm when your soul is overcome by memories of their last moments.

2. GROUNDING YOURSELF WHEN MEMORIES TORMENT YOU

Trauma can be tormenting; it can completely take over. Trauma is not only what happened to you, it's the aftermath of what happened. It's how our spirit, soul, body, mind, and nervous system try to make sense of what just happened. Trauma can affect every aspect of our being and can show up in a variety of ways: depression, anxiety, nervousness, sickness, etc.

Sometimes while in training, I was triggered. Sometimes, I'd have to revisit things that were extremely hard. For many professionals, out of nowhere, working with others can unearth some trauma lying dormant. Flashbacks or painful images would take over.

My uncle, who was like a brother to me, was in ICU for a month. Our family lived day in and day out on a roller coaster, and the last week of his life, we watched his body wind down until his final moments. This is called **Anticipatory Grief**. Anticipatory grief is experienced before a loss happens, such as when a loved one is terminally ill, aging, or declining. It is all the losses and fears felt before the death actually occurs.

Not only were my dreams shattered from a great family reunion with him and the remainder of my family I had hoped for, but I also extended my faith, only to have God say no, which shattered me in disappointment.

I had nightmares for months from the trauma of watching my best friend since childhood slowly pass and take his last breath. What I've learned is that we're not meant to carry these traumatic losses alone. There are qualified professionals to help us navigate this. God sent professionals trained to assist us in navigating the unbearable grief we carry.

I've also learned to do something over and over again expecting a different result is called insanity. For years, I was stuck in some of my **Old Wounds**, with my past pains and traumas creeping into the present. I believed that you can pray everything away, but things weren't changing for me. I was trying to pray my trauma away, but it came to a point where I had to accept I needed more help than just prayer alone. Even in my prayer time, I still wasn't processing my pain and needed help navigating these wounds.

God sent us people that can actually assist Him in helping us. Yes, Jesus can fix it all, but for some things, it'll take Jesus and assigned helpers to get us through these tough moments.

Shortly after my uncle passed, it was the turning point where I started therapy. Between all the losses, and that loss that tipped me over, I got help. That truly broke everything in me, where I felt like I was going down a deep, dark hole with nobody able to save me.

Getting help for my trauma changed my life and was a turning point in ending the cycle of suffering I was in. It literally got me on my path toward healing, which is why I am able to write to you today. I've heard countless stories of horrific things people's loved ones have gone through, and like me, you just can't shake it.

I had to get tools to help me process these memories that would take over. I'd like to share with you one technique to help bring your mind gently back to the present. When this occurs, I gently invite you to try this:

The 5-4-3-2-1 Technique:

- Look around you; name five things you see.
- Notice four things you can touch and feel.
- Identify three things you hear.
- Notice two things you can smell.
- Focus on one thing you can taste.

Breathe slowly and deeply. **Grounding** helps to allow your awareness to return to this moment, where you are safe. Then gently ask yourself:

- What does your belief system or faith say they are right now?
- Are they still suffering at this moment, or are they free from pain?

Right now, being grounded and mindful where you are, what does your faith say about them? Grounding brings your thoughts back to the moment where you are when your mind wants to pull you back to what was. This is key. This technique is bringing you back into the now. More importantly, it's bringing your loved one back to the now too, where you're both safe.

If by faith you believe, I pray you can hold on to these truths:

- Your loved one is free from that traumatic moment.
- They will never have to relive that pain ever again.

Again, I'm not certain of your loss, and I'm so sorry for your pain. I know it's unbearable that it ended that way. My heart is broken and I am so sorry. But while we can't change what happened, I pray God will anchor you in this truth:

- They are safe.
- They are held.
- They are loved.
- They are free from hurt or harm.

You'll never understand it. You'll never be okay with it. This reflection isn't meant to erase the tragedy or to make sense of any of it. I know your life is forever changed and you'll never be okay with your loss.

For right now, it's simply an invitation to press deeper into faith, even with your questions, your anger, and your shattered heart. It is to help you find an anchor in the midst of the storm when your heart and mind race out of control and won't let you rest. Christ Jesus is your rock. He is a firm place where you can lock in when the world around you is dark, scary, lonely, lost, and out of control. Allow Him to be your anchor in the midst of the storm.

God understands. He can take it. Give Him your questions, your rage, your heartbreak. He is still God. He can handle it.

I know for most, the questions remain:

- Is my loved one safe?
- Are they at peace?
- Are they being taken care of?
- Where is their soul now?

When we don't have the answers to those questions, trust God! He is the author and finisher of our lives, and He has our loved ones too. Everyone has their own relationship with God, even if we don't know it. In our loved one's final hours, you don't know how God in Christ Jesus appeared to them, spoke to them, or what they uttered to God before they passed.

When you question where they are, remember the thief on the cross with Jesus. Just before he died, Jesus appealed to him and promised he would be with Him in paradise (Luke 23:39–43, NIV). God is sovereign, loving, kind, forgiving, and merciful, even when we don't deserve it. Remind yourself of that and let God comfort you that all things are reconciled in heaven. He has your loved one in His hand.

He's got them, and He's got you. I'm so sorry you've gone through what you've gone through. I'm sending you so much love right now, right where you hurt.

I love you and I'm thinking about you.

With love,
Ke'Shawn

SCRIPTURE

"He will wipe every tear from their eyes. There will be no more death or mourning or crying or pain, for the old order of things has passed away" (**Revelation 21:4, NIV**).

"Peace I leave with you; my peace I give you. I do not give to you as the world gives. Do not let your hearts be troubled and do not be afraid" (**John 14:27, NIV**).

"The Lord is my rock, my fortress and my deliverer; my God is my rock, in whom I take refuge, my shield and the horn of my salvation, my stronghold" (**Psalm 18:2, NIV**).

REFLECTION

What God allows in this lifetime sometimes is unbearable. Our loved ones are gone way too soon. I thank The Lord for Jesus, that when life is unbearable, trauma happens, and tragedy strikes, Jesus has overcome the world. He holds the keys to death. Once we leave here to go be with Him, I'm comforted to know the old order of things in this world passes away along with all the pain. We get to walk with God in the cool of the day, to be with Him and those who have gone before us.

Does it take away the grief? Absolutely not. Do we want them still with us? Absolutely. But since that decision wasn't up to us, I thank God for Jesus, that there will be a great reunion according to our Christian faith.

It's not goodbye, it's "I'll see you again, my beloved. Save a seat for me." God Himself promises an end to pain and suffering. What took your loved one's life no longer has authority or power over them. God has made all things new for them.

No more crying.

No more pain.

No more worry.

No more sadness.

They are free.

They are whole.

They are safe in His presence forever.

Whenever you're ready, let this truth slowly meet you right where you are. There is no rush. It'll take time, but allow the joy of seeing them again to give you a reason to keep holding on.

REFLECTION QUESTIONS

1. What moments or images from your loved one's passing replay in your mind?
2. How does it feel to know that your loved one is now completely free from pain and suffering?
3. What truth from your faith can you hold on to today to quiet the torment in your soul?

PRAYER

Father, in the name of Jesus, I pray that Your truth will wash over me like a quiet river. Bring supernatural comfort and tenderly replace the torment replaying in my soul with peace. Hold me steady as I wrestle with my questions, my heartbreak, and my anger. Help me believe that my loved one is free, safe, and whole in Your presence.

I tear down every thought, every imagination, every lie of the enemy, every thought of my past, and bring it to the obedience of Christ. I clothe myself with the mind of Christ. I will think on things that are true, that are right, that are lovely, excellent, praiseworthy; those things that are of good report. I have the mind of Christ.

Lord Jesus, thank You for taking over my mind and bringing me back to this moment, allowing Your peace, Your shalom, to fall on me. To know that my loved one is safe in You, and I believe it, Father God, even if my heart, my mind, and my soul quake within me, I submit to You right now.

I ask that You take over what has taken over me, Father God, and let shalom be my portion in the land of the living. Let me rest in You. Father God, bring me to an expected end, where there's peace and rest and I can sleep.

Hold me in the hollow of Your hands when my tragedy has taken over. You stand before me and say, "Peace, be still," and I receive Your peace.

In Jesus' mighty name, Amen.

DAY 6
JOURNAL

_____

_____

_____

_____

_____

_____

_____

_____

_____

_____

_____

_____

_____

_____

_____

_____

_____

_____

_____

_____

_____

_____

_____

_____

How Are You Today? Really?

If you're grieving, the honest answer might be simple: What do you think? I just lost my loved one. Terrible! But I'm not asking in general. Most people are not asking in general.

Right now, at this very moment, what feelings are coming up for you? How are you really doing? And what do you need?

After our loved ones pass, this question, "How are you?", becomes common, and honestly, sometimes it can feel infuriating: "What do you mean, how am I? My loved one just died. How do you think I am?" I've learned over the years that most people mean well. They ask because they're awkward, unsure what to say, and most times, they truly want to know.

They're not asking how you are overall. They already know you're heartbroken. What they really mean is:

- How are you right now?
- How are you in this moment?
- How are you holding up today?

Depending on the person and the moment, your answer might be brutally honest:

"I feel like my life is falling apart."

"I feel like I'm dying."

And sometimes, if we're really honest, "I want to die too!"

I've sat with many people, and depending on who they lost, those are real emotions. If at any time you contemplate self-harm, please call **911 or 988** for immediate assistance. It's okay to not be okay.

For others, it might be something lighter, like:

"I'm doing okay."

"I'm not okay!"

"I'm managing."

Because not everyone we want to let in deserves our true, authentic story. We have to feel safe to share how we really feel. So, when people ask, try not to be angry. People are concerned and are just checking on you.

BEYOND THE QUESTIONS FROM OTHERS

Here's the part we often miss: we need to ask ourselves that same question. We need to check in with ourselves.

- How am I today?
- What do I need right now?
- What can I do in this moment to meet that need?
- How can I let others know what I need?

As a mom, I used to automatically say "tired" whenever someone asked how I was doing. That became my story, my go-to response. But when I finally paused and checked in with myself, I realized sometimes I wasn't even tired. I was in a fog, moving on autopilot. "Tired" was my label, but it wasn't always true at the moment. It was my story, my narrative, my go-to. But when I checked my heart, sometimes I really wasn't tired. It was what I told myself because it had become a norm.

Grief works like that too. It changes moment to moment. There are times when you feel overwhelmed, moments when you break, but there are also small, quiet pockets where, for just a heartbeat, you're simply okay, stable, and focused.

Today, I invite you to pause and check in with your own heart:

- How am I doing right now?
- What do I need in this moment?
- What can I do to give myself that care?

Checking in with yourself is an act of self-love and self-care, and if you can, share what you discover with someone you trust. People want to support you but often don't know how. Sometimes we don't know either until we stop and listen to our own heart.

When you do, you might be surprised by what you find. You'll begin to understand your grief in a new way, and you'll be able to guide others to meet you right where you are.

So today, give yourself a little love. Pause. Check in. I'm checking on you too. How are you doing right now?

I love you and I'm thinking about you.

With love,
Ke'Shawn

SCRIPTURE

"Come to me, all you who are weary and burdened, and I will give you rest" (**Matthew 11:28, NIV**).

REFLECTION

Sitting still in quiet may feel impossible right now. The silence can feel too heavy, too loud. But just for a few seconds, come to The Lord. Check in with yourself and simply receive. Little by little, you'll find you can sit a little longer, and in that stillness, He will meet you, giving you what you need in this very moment.

REFLECTION QUESTIONS

1. Right now, at this very moment, how are you truly feeling?
2. What do you need today, emotionally, spiritually, or physically?
3. Is there someone you can share your current feelings and needs with?
4. How can you show yourself kindness in this moment of grief?

PRAYER

Father, in the name of Jesus, I feel all over the place right now. I'm high, I'm low, I have every emotion under the sun; sometimes rage, sometimes pure sadness. Only You can stabilize me. You meet me exactly where I am, and everything I'm feeling is okay. Give me inner peace, Lord. Let me know deep inside that I will be okay.

Tonight, allow me to rest in You. Grant me peaceful sleep, refresh my weary soul, and hold me steady in Your arms.

In Jesus' mighty name, Amen.

DAY 7
JOURNAL

_____
_____
_____
_____
_____
_____
_____
_____
_____
_____
_____
_____
_____
_____
_____
_____
_____
_____
_____
_____
_____
_____
_____
_____
_____
_____

Busy Is My Solitude, and That's Okay!

I remember the day my mom and I were told by the doctors in the hospital that my dad had passed. Everything in me collapsed, and in that moment, every hope I had for him to live died with him. After the initial shock, my mind automatically went into survival mode: "OK, what do I need to do?"

I shifted straight into **Task Mode**: a state where you focus on doing instead of feeling. You put complete focus on what needs to be done because slowing down feels like the grief will swallow you whole. In this state, you don't have time to feel; it's too much to do.

We cook. We clean. We organize. We plan. We make lists. We take care of everyone else.

We're busy because we don't have a choice. For most of us, we stay busy because the thought of sitting in silence feels unbearable. That same day, I went straight to Bed Bath & Beyond. My thoughts were already racing: We'll have to tell people. Guests will soon fill the house. We need to prepare.

We had a thousand phone calls to make and arrangements to handle. There was no pause to think about what I needed. No time to let the pain in. Life didn't stop so I could grieve. Straight from the hospital, my mom and I spent hours preparing for guests and what was next. That busyness lasted for weeks, until the funeral and post-funeral.

Truthfully, I avoided silence because I was terrified of it. I couldn't bear the thought of being still, especially with God in prayer. I knew if I sat too long with my feelings, the weight of that pain might crush me.

Do you find yourself here too, staying busy to survive because the silence feels too heavy? Please hear me: that's okay. Sometimes grief looks like endless motion. Sometimes survival means staying on your feet. There will come a day when you'll be able to sit longer, to be quiet, to let God hold all the feelings you're avoiding right now. But until then, you're doing what you can to make it through.

While you're in this survival season, take small pockets of care for yourself: Drink water. Keep a nutritional shake nearby to keep your strength up. Have a snack within reach. Pause for just a few seconds to breathe. If sleep won't come, consider a natural supplement to gently help your body rest.

No one can tell you how to grieve. People around you may try to guide or protect you, and they truly mean well. Let them help where they can, but also give yourself permission to say: "This is what I need to survive right now."

People may judge your busy as avoidance, but that's the furthest thing from the truth. Our body has its own wisdom. When it's time to deal with something, our body and soul will dictate what it needs. Also, don't allow anyone to push you, or tell you you're grieving wrong.

If you're like me, you may have fears going into the presence of God for the moment or avoiding prayer. Sometimes we're consumed with emotions. Sometimes we're trying to process what just happened or what God allowed to happen, and we avoid praying. Prayer is what we need the most.

Going into His presence is the only thing that will heal us, but The Lord understands where we find ourselves, our hearts broken and hope crushed. He will lead us back to Him when our hearts grow quiet and cold for the moment. He accepts and embraces us right where we are.

It's okay not to be ready to face those big emotions, so in the meantime, it's okay to JUST BE. Right after I left the hospital, my coping was just getting things done. I shed a few tears at the hospital, but I wiped them, picked myself up by the bootstraps, and focused.

While at Bed Bath & Beyond, I scurried, finding some of the things we needed. It wasn't until I couldn't find a kitchen hand towel that I broke. That was the straw that broke the camel's back. I searched and searched and got so angry, "Where are the hand towels?" The customer service rep told me, "Sorry ma'am, we ran out!"

I was infuriated, and while waiting in line, I literally burst. I quietly started crying, then quickly, I started sobbing in line, where everyone was watching me. The customers and cashier said, "OMG, are you okay?" I said as I sobbed, "I just came from the hospital. My father died 30 minutes ago."

My body did exactly what it needed at that moment, without my permission. My lack of sitting and feeling wasn't avoidance, it was my body's way of protecting me for the moment because the feelings I was feeling were more than I could handle. Sometimes, the emotions from grief can feel like a tsunami coming to consume and overtake us, and the thought of it can be terrifying. That's okay too. The pain is beyond words. I don't know your specific loss, but I feel led to encourage you, whatever you are feeling, I'm reminded of the Scripture:

"God is within you; you will not fall. God will help you at break of day." (Psalm 46:5, NIV, paraphrased)

You are doing fine. Allow yourself to just be and don't force yourself to do anything, and as time passes, everything will slowly settle. You'll find yourself craving quiet moments of rest. Until then, I'm praying that even in your busyness, the peace of God will rest on you, soothing your soul as you keep moving forward.

I love you. I'm thinking of you and your self-care today.

With love,
Ke'Shawn

SCRIPTURE

"Come, all you who are thirsty, come to the waters; and you who have no money, come, buy and eat!...Listen, listen to me, and eat what is good, and you will delight in the richest of fare" (**Isaiah 55:1–2, NIV**).

REFLECTION

The Lord doesn't need anything from you, only that you come. His hands are already extended, waiting to pour into you and give you what you need. Even if you can't sit in silence for long, even if you can't find the words to pray, take just a few seconds to pause. Hold your hands open and whisper:

"Lord, I receive Your comfort.

I receive Your peace.

I receive Your rest.

I receive Your grace, courage, and strength to sit and be still in Your presence."

Allow The Lord to pour into you. He'll give you what you need in the moment. Little by little, this simple act will strengthen your soul and teach your spirit to rest.

REFLECTION QUESTIONS

- When you think about Task Mode, what does it look like for you?
- How can you care for your body and soul while staying busy?
- Who can you ask to help carry the load so you're not doing everything alone?

PRAYER

Father, I pray for the courage to sit in silence, even if only for a millisecond, so I may receive strength to carry me from moment to moment. When I don't have the courage to pray or to face my feelings, I thank You that You already know what I need, and You will give it to me.

Holy Spirit, communicate my deepest needs to the Father and meet me where I am. Thank You that no matter what, You will not allow me to be consumed. In my greatest fears, You will not let me fall.

I'm afraid to feel. I may never stop crying. I'm afraid if I allow the emotions to flow, it will break me. But Your Word says I will not be broken. You will hold me up and give me a firm place to stand.

I trust You and give You my fears, because I'm wrecked in fear. Quiet my fears with Your love. Thank You for being a God who is all-knowing, who intimately knows me even when I'm not speaking. Help me create pockets of time to slow down. Allow me to pace myself and find true rest when I need it most.

I pray for peaceful sleep tonight, and I thank You for it. In Jesus' mighty name, Amen.

DAY 8
JOURNAL

_____

_____

_____

_____

_____

_____

_____

_____

_____

_____

_____

_____

_____

_____

_____

_____

_____

_____

_____

_____

_____

_____

_____

_____

_____

I'm Tired!

"I'm tired!" That's become my daily phrase since becoming a mom. As a stay-at-home mom, wife, entrepreneur, in ministry, daughter, best friend, and sister, etc., I'm always on the move. There's always something to do, always someone or something that needs my attention. There's never a dull moment.

So, when I say, "I'm tired," I mean it; I'm truly, physically tired.

But when grief entered my life, I discovered a different kind of tired. Since the age of seven, I've lost so many loved ones, year after year, loss after loss. Over time, my soul became exhausted in a way no nap, no day off, no full night of sleep could fix. Grief alone can drain your entire being. Not to mention, my sleep patterns changed.

My REM sleep was down to 30 minutes a night, and the remaining time I spent in twilight always sleeping on alert. Between becoming a parent and grief, my sleep hadn't truly been sweet. This isn't just feeling sleepy.

This is **soul-tired:** a deep, aching weariness that comes from heartbreak, loss, and trying to hold yourself together when life has fallen apart. It's a state of high alert, never being able to rest, because we're preparing for the next disaster. Do you feel that right now? Not just physically worn out, but exhausted to the core of your soul?

The truth is, grief is exhausting! If you're in grief, I know you're tired. I know your soul is weary. I know you need more than physical rest, you need rest for your soul.

I remember one day taking a shower, and after coming out, I sat on the edge of my couch in my bedroom. I instantly became so tired; not physically, but my soul, out of nowhere, felt like it was literally collapsing. At any moment, I felt like I was checking out. I knew, right then and there, if I didn't do something differently, physically, my body wouldn't last the weight of my soul being so crushed and exhausted.

I waited too long to find rest, and my nervous system always being on "10" is straight unhealthy for spirit, soul, and body. I came to the end of myself. In prayer, The Lord revealed to me that I wasn't resting in my soul. I was so busy trying to keep up with my life and hold grief simultaneously, I was drowning. So, I started sleeping more, which helped, but He taught me this: Ke'Shawn, you need rest for your soul.

Then, I began a new journey of how to rest in my soul. During this process, I've learned that I can rest in God by learning to trust Him in the midst of the storms, the stressors, and the busyness of life. I had to learn how to trust Him again after being disappointed, having life ripped from underneath me. I had to learn again how to trust His decision-making and His sovereignty, His strength, and His ability to handle what I cannot control.

I had to learn to surrender to the moments, and trust that as Abba Father, I'm safe. That's a big deal in grief: being safe. To learn to trust Him again. To learn how to surrender to His will, knowing I was going to be safe no matter what. It's in those moments of surrender that my soul starts to heal.

Today, I invite you to surrender too.

Sometimes our souls are weary from enduring trials, but other times they're weary because we've been trying to control everything after our lives have shattered. Lean back into His sovereignty. Your life, and the life of your loved one, is in His hands.

So, how can we find this rest?

By leaning into His Word. After loss, our souls are shattered and our fears expand. Our nervous system goes into constant **fight-or-flight**, 24 hours a day, 7 days a week. How do we get to a place of true rest in the middle of the storm? By learning in quietness to sit in His presence. By leaning into soaking worship music or instrumentals to help soothe us in quietness.

By surrounding yourself with the Word of God, playing the audio Bible, finding playlists of Scripture on YouTube, and listening to or spending time with His Word, I found that the Psalms brought me comfort. Listening to prayers I found on YouTube also helped when I couldn't find the words to pray for myself.

I started journaling, to allow my feelings and fears to find a home and to make sense of things. I also decided to get help. I went to therapy to help me manage the enormity of my life. Sometimes, we allow the weight of our stressors, grief, and life responsibilities to go too far. Sometimes, we just need a safe place to let it all out.

During this time of profound grief, you lose your footing. It's important we have an arsenal of tools to assist us in stabilizing ourselves and positioning ourselves to allow God to give us rest; not just physical rest, but soul rest.

Death makes us fearful, so we must be reaffirmed, planting our feet again in trusting His sovereignty and protection. To know from Him: we are safe, we are loved, we are protected. Despite the boat capsizing, He will not allow us to drown. He will grab us with an out-stretched arm and save us, causing us to rest in Him. He is Abba, Father, and only He can cause us to truly rest.

I love you and I'm thinking about you.

With love,
Ke'Shawn

SCRIPTURE

"Even youths grow tired and weary, and young men stumble and fall; but those who hope in The Lord will renew their strength. They will soar on wings like eagles; they will run and not grow weary, they will walk and not faint" (**Isaiah 40:30–31, NIV**).

REFLECTION

When your soul feels like a dry desert wasteland, there is a place you can go: into the presence of God. He alone can water and revive your soul. It doesn't have to be long. If you can't sit still for minutes, start with seconds. Find tiny pockets of time to escape, lift your hands, and whisper:

"Lord, I receive Your rest and renewal."

Little by little, He will fill you up again.

REFLECTION QUESTIONS

- What can you do right now to soothe your weary soul?
- How can you keep filling your cup when life keeps emptying it out?
- What do you need most right now, and how can you let others, or God Himself, help meet that need?

PRAYER

Father, I'm tired. My soul is exhausted and weary, and I'm coming to You for rest. It's not the kind of rest the world gives, but the rest only You can provide. I breathe in Your life, Your grace, and Your strength. I breathe out my exhaustion, my heaviness. I lay it all at Your feet. Lord, I'm afraid and I can't rest.

Allow me to be settled that You are Father, and You've got me. You will not allow me to be overtaken. Allow peace, like a river, to rest upon me. I receive Your supernatural peace. Renew me, Lord. Refresh me.

In Jesus' mighty name, Amen.

DAY 9
JOURNAL

_____
_____
_____
_____
_____
_____
_____
_____
_____
_____
_____
_____
_____
_____
_____
_____
_____
_____
_____
_____
_____
_____
_____
_____
_____

When Disappointments Feel Like Betrayal

*L*ife doesn't stop because you had a death in your family. Responsibilities don't care that your loved one just died; they demand immediate attention. I found in my grieving process just how insensitive and unfair this part of life can be. My life had fallen to pieces, yet I was expected to just move on. I was dying inside, but the world around me laughed and experienced joy while I was trapped in a bubble.

This part of grief made me enraged. People made me enraged, and I just wasn't here for it. Grief had my patience shot and my tolerance for any type of shenanigans at an all-time low.

I remember after my dad died, I was managing an office. While planning his funeral, I still had to go to work, making sure my team was taken care of before I took time off. But even then, the phone calls kept coming in about things that could have waited.

I remember not feeling supported by the institution I had served for over five years, an institution I had poured my blood, sweat, and tears into. When I was in my deepest need, my loss wasn't acknowledged. It was as though my dad's death didn't matter.

I would go into meetings silent, there in body but completely checked out in spirit and mind. I was starting to become bitter. If it weren't for God, if it weren't for me choosing to stay faithful to Him through my work, I would have walked away.

It was my assignment from God to be there, so I couldn't leave. I also had bills. I had responsibilities, and life, as cruel as it felt, just went on. That made me enraged.

Sometimes, at work, you'll have amazing people who rally around you, hug you, and give you whatever you need. If that's your story, thank God. That is a gift from heaven. But for others like me, we live and work in a **grief-illiterate** culture, one that lacks compassion and empathy for those carrying invisible wounds. Even now, after the pandemic, while there's been much progress, there's still so much more work to be done.

I'll never forget when a VP asked my boss, "What's wrong with her? She seems angry." And my supervisor had my back and responded, "She is angry. She just lost her father." There was a total disconnect. No understanding. No space to simply be broken.

It's not just work. It's also the insensitivity of words people speak, thinking they're comforting us but really making things worse. It's people avoiding you because your grief and loss make them uncomfortable. It's not having enough time to grieve before you're forced back into a world that feels foreign and harsh. It's going back to work just to be on autopilot, completely checked out.

It's the lack of support sometimes, the feeling of people just not showing up. All of this feels like betrayal. Grief already feels so isolating, like you're on a desert island with no one in sight. To add insult to injury is when people don't show up, it truly feels like abandonment and betrayal.

This betrayal I'm speaking of is not always intentional. I've come to learn that we truly live in a grief-illiterate culture where people don't understand how to truly care for the grieving. They literally don't get it until they've walked it, and for that, we can't fully blame them.

So when I use the word betrayal, I don't mean everyone intentionally abandoned or hurt us. But the disappointment is real, the pain is real, and it cuts deep. Today, I just want to acknowledge that pain.

I want to say I'm sorry. I'm sorry for everyone that has hurt you while you were in your deepest need. I'm sorry for every time you felt abandoned or unsupported. I'm sorry for every time you felt betrayed by people you thought would show up but didn't. I'm sorry that life demands so much when you have nothing left to give.

Though we can't change what others did or didn't do, we can begin to release that pain and let God heal the places people couldn't reach. Over time, I learned that to move past the rage, I had to lower my expectations of people.

I had to remind myself:

- Sometimes, people truly don't know what to do.
- Some people simply aren't equipped to show up the way we need.
- And sometimes, God Himself is protecting us from those who might cause deeper harm.
- Sometimes, the people we're expecting to show up for us are simply not assigned by God to support us in that season.

- Sometimes, God wants to be our main support, and He will weed out others so that we can solely lean on Him.
- Sometimes, trials allow us to see better what types of friends and family we have in our circle and what category they belong in for our lives, so we're not disappointed when they don't show up how we're expecting.

For example, you have your ride-or-die. They show up no matter what. Social friends are just good to hang out with. You have friends that you don't speak to all the time and who are not a part of your everyday life, but are great for emergencies. You have your takers. They aren't able to pour into your cup, period! Your confidant, that great listener. You get the picture?

Not every family member or friend is there to hold you down, so do yourself a favor and don't expect it. Know exactly how they show up in your life, accept them how they are and leave it there. If that relationship no longer serves you well and doesn't reciprocate, then you have something to pray about regarding their role in your life.

I had to lean completely on God, trusting Him one millisecond at a time. I had to learn to ask for help, communicate my needs, and take days off for my soul's survival.

So today, I gently encourage you:
- Take people off the hook.
- Forgive where you can.
- Let go of the expectations you have of others that only deepen your disappointment.

This doesn't mean what they did, or didn't do, was okay. It means you're choosing to protect your own heart.

Today, I see you. My heart is breaking with yours, and my prayer is that The Lord will bring you angels in human form to comfort, support, and guide you as you navigate this wilderness and help you find peace.

I love you and I'm thinking about you.

With love,
Ke'Shawn

SCRIPTURE

"I will not leave you as orphans; I will come to you" (**John 14:18, NIV**).

"Though my father and mother forsake me, The Lord will receive me" (**Psalm 27:10, NIV**).

"Though the mountains be shaken and the hills be removed, yet my unfailing love for you will not be shaken nor my covenant of peace be removed, says The Lord, who has compassion on you" (**Isaiah 54:10, NIV**).

REFLECTION

The Lord is constant, unchanging, and consistent. When others fail you, God won't ever. In moments when you feel abandoned or overlooked, remember this truth: you are never alone. He sees you. He understands your pain when no one else does. No height or depth will separate Him from you. His love will consume you.

When the world changes, He will absolutely remain the same, constantly caring for you and making provision for you.

As you grieve, also take a moment to notice and appreciate anyone who has shown you kindness, even in small ways, it's a reminder that God is still sending comfort through human hands.

REFLECTION QUESTIONS

- What has disappointed you most in your grieving process regarding how people showed up?
- What would it look like to forgive those who didn't meet your expectations?
- What support do you need right now, and how can you begin seeking it from others or directly from God?

PRAYER

Father, I feel so disappointed, abandoned, and unseen. I release every person who didn't show up for me the way I hoped. I forgive them, and I give this burden to You. I forgive them as You have forgiven me. The hurt is real. It does feel like betrayal. I'm angry and enraged sometimes about how I'm handled. Have mercy on them and have mercy on me.

I release them to You right now. Speak to their hearts. Speak to my heart and help me to remember that I lack perfection. Although I may think I've always shown up for others, there have been times in my life I've disappointed others too.

Help me to extend grace. Forgive them, for they know not what they do. Allow the spirit of peace to allow me to be a peacemaker with all men and to position myself to forgive.

I choose to forgive right now, and I breathe and release them to You. I let them go in Jesus' name. Lord, send the right people at the right time. Send angels who will carry me when I cannot walk. Thank You for never leaving me or forsaking me. Thank You for the support I've been given, even the smallest acts of kindness are gifts from You.

I thank You, and I appreciate and love You.

In Jesus' mighty name, Amen.

DAY 10
JOURNAL

_____

_____

_____

_____

_____

_____

_____

_____

_____

_____

_____

_____

_____

_____

_____

_____

_____

_____

_____

_____

_____

_____

_____

_____

_____

_____

When God's Answer Is "No"

At the age of seven, I lost my grandmother. From there, I had **Cumulative Loss.** Year after year, I experienced loss after loss, one by one, not catching a break in between. Cumulative loss is when multiple losses happen over time, often before you have had a chance to heal from the previous ones.

I remember one night, my mother and I were on our knees, getting ready to pray before bed. We started talking about my Uncle Danny and how suddenly he had passed. I absolutely loved and adored my Uncle Danny and relished every moment I had with him. He was my grandmother's oldest brother and the patriarch of the family. He was our family glue. I would pretend to be sick at school, knowing he was my emergency pick-up, just so I could be with him and my Aunt Gloria.

One moment he was with us, and the next, he was gone. I could always depend on my Uncle Danny. He was a strong, dependable tower after losing my grandmother. As a child, I felt helpless with the constant deaths. I understood the fragility of life and how quickly everything could change. One moment we're here, and the next, we're not.

I remember my mother and I were on our knees, getting ready to pray. She looked at me and said, "That's why it's so important that you pray for people and for your family. Your prayers have the power to save someone's life!" She continued, "As my mother taught me, if you have legs and can walk, get on your knees and pray. Honor God. Get on your knees and pray. Pray for your family! Your prayers can help save someone's life!"

As a kid, that changed everything for me. Little ole me? Do you mean to tell me that I have some sort of power to pray, and perhaps my prayers can save someone's life? Do you mean I have the ability to stop death in its tracks? OMG, that one thing out of many changed my life. That was the day the seed of intercession was born in my life.

As a kid, I took that to heart and I began to pray without ceasing. I prayed when I woke up, prayed throughout the day for my family. I prayed all the time, everywhere I went. Not just for my family, but strangers too. I understood that the final decision was up to God, and that I couldn't force God to do anything just because I prayed, but it allowed me to understand that my prayers had power. I believed what my Mommy told me.

We weren't religious people, but faith, prayer, and the Bible were important to our family. I thought, If I should pray, it can help save someone's life!

Fast forward to me as an adult. I remember praying to God: "Lord, I've lost so many people. Please, just don't take my mom and my dad, Pete. Let them see me get married, have children, and enjoy life together. Please, please, I've had to accept everyone else You've taken. Don't take them. Lord, if You take my parents, You and I are going to have some serious problems."

I meant that with every fiber of my being. I tolerated God's decision, but I can't say I wasn't salty for Him taking everyone else. But that would be the last straw for me with Him taking my people.

Then came the day that broke me. I was awakened one early Saturday morning by my mom saying that my dad wouldn't wake up. She kept saying, "He won't wake up." I went into the room, and just like she said, he was unresponsive. Instead of panicking, I did what I knew to do in faith, what she taught me, I started praying. I anointed his body with oil and declared with everything in me: "He shall live and not die and see the salvation of The Lord!"

The EMTs came and worked on him. As they worked, I kept decreeing and declaring: "He shall live and not die!" I believed. I stood in faith.

We got to the hospital. An hour passed and they were still working on him. They were working on him for a while, and I kept decreeing and declaring: "He shall live and not die and see the salvation of The Lord!" I stood firm and believed! I knew he was going to walk out of that room.

Then, I saw everyone leaving the room. The main doctor came to us and told us to be seated. I refused. He said, "I'm sorry, we did everything we could. Your husband, your father, has passed. I'm so sorry."

At that moment, what I told God before, "If You take my mother or father, Pete, we're going to have some serious problems," flashed across my mind.

All I could do was look up to heaven and whisper, "Lord, I love You still. I love You, still," as I sobbed. I continued to say, "I have no other place to go. I love You, still!"

I realized in that moment, what I was really saying to God previously was that by Him taking either of my parents, that would destroy my relationship with Him. But in that moment, at the crossroads of my faith, I knew: There is no other God who can heal me how He can. There is no other God who can love me how He can. There is no other God who can save me how He did.

I had tried everything under the sun to comfort my heart through all of my bereavements, and nothing worked but God in Jesus Christ Himself. Right there, I stood at a crossroad. Do I abandon my faith or do I trust Him while my heart is shattered? Maybe you've had many prayers you've prayed, just like me, and you were utterly disappointed when God's answer was "no."

Was I angry with God? Yes. Did I love Him with everything in me? Yes. Was I disappointed in His decision-making? Absolutely. Was I salty and bitter with Him? Absolutely! After all, I prayed the prayer that he should live and not die and see the salvation of The Lord, and my dad still died. I know I'm not the only one that has experienced anger and disappointment with God when His answer was "no."

I sit with you in that disappointment. I'm so sorry for every time you exercised your faith and were left shattered by God's "no." God reminded me in Scripture: "My ways are not your ways, and My thoughts are not your thoughts."

Sometimes we think we're asking for a fish, but we're really asking for a snake. Sometimes God sees what we can't see. Even when we think our loved one should still be alive, we don't see the bigger picture, the plans of the enemy, the pain they may have faced if they lived.

It's in His sovereignty that I've had to dig deep and trust Him. I'm sorry if your heart is shattered because God said "no." Every day, not only do you deal with their deaths, but what about all the secondary losses? It's just not fair, I know! But I want you to know this: He loves you with an unyielding, reckless, undying love. Even in the middle of disappointment, He has not left you.

I want to encourage you. I know you're disappointed, I know you may feel hopeless, but I implore you, don't let go. Believe again to see what the end may be. Our faith, especially when life throws its most terrible curveballs, when the enemy roars and comes at you and your family in tumultuous ways, will be challenged.

Our faith may grow weak and diminish. This is the moment where the rubber meets the road in our faith, where we have to choose what we truly believe. It's the place where the Bible has to become real. It's a place where you have to decide and work the Word, believe the Word, trust what God says. His plans for our life and our loved ones are for good, not evil, to bring us to a good end.

I love you and I'm thinking about you.

With love,
Ke'Shawn

SCRIPTURE

"My thoughts are not your thoughts, neither are your ways My ways, declares The Lord. As the heavens are higher than the earth, so are My ways higher than your ways and My thoughts than your thoughts" (**Isaiah 55:8–9, NIV**).

"I am the Alpha and the Omega, the Beginning and the End" (**Revelation 22:13, NIV**).

"For I know the thoughts that I think toward you, saith The Lord, thoughts of peace, and not of evil, to give you an expected end" (**Jeremiah 29:11, KJV**).

REFLECTION

You may be angry with God right now, and that's okay. You may not want to talk to Him at all, and that's okay too. He welcomes your anger. He can handle your frustration. He knows your disappointments. He knows that your hope feels crushed and your heart feels sick.

Give it all to Him. He can carry it. He's capable of wrestling with you and will not let you go. I know sometimes what happens isn't fair. I know some things are unexplainable.

Today, what do you believe? If you walk away from your faith, where will you go? What God can truly heal you? Despite the worst things happening, He is still good, He cares, He's still God. Don't let go of God in Jesus Christ! You can't see it now, but one day, it will get clearer, and each moment you trust Him, He's healing you. He is bringing you to an expected end.

REFLECTION QUESTIONS

- In what areas has God's "no" crushed your heart?
- How has this loss impacted your faith?
- What can you do to begin rebuilding your faith and keeping the embers alive?
- Where has The Lord brought you from that can help you reflect, remind, and restore your faith in His healing power of your past?

PRAYER

Father, in the name of Jesus, I'm broken. I'm angry, and I'm disappointed. I believed that You could save my loved one, and You didn't. I believed my life consisted of having my loved one, and we would enjoy life together and have a great future, and You didn't follow through.

Father, I can't lie or hide from You, but I'm angry You took my loved one. I'm angry at what I will no longer have. I'm angry about my crushed dreams and the future we no longer get to create together. I'm angry because really, I'm super sad and hurting.

My faith too is weak and weary, and parts of me died too. My hope is weak and faint, sometimes broken. I give You my broken heart, and I pray in the name of Jesus that the fire, even if it's nothing more than embers, will never burn out. I don't want to lose my faith. That I too won't die with them. That You will breathe in me again, and again, and again.

Meet me in my dreams and my sleep and revive my soul again. Resurrect the faith that feels like it's dying.

Visit me while I'm sleeping to comfort me and reassure me that You did hear me.

Don't let this loss make me bitter. Make me better. Turn my pain into purpose. Help me continue to share Your love with people and keep my love for You alive. Don't let me die, help me to believe again and forgive me if in my pain, I have dishonored You.

I do love You, I'm just angry sometimes. Forgive me and have mercy on this weak vessel. I need You, and I don't want to abandon my faith. I receive Your life and breathe again.

In Jesus' mighty name, Amen.

DAY 11
JOURNAL

_____

_____

_____

_____

_____

_____

_____

_____

_____

_____

_____

_____

_____

_____

_____

_____

_____

_____

_____

_____

_____

Your Tears Matter

ver the last couple of years, I've entered a season, in my 40s, where many of my peers are either helping to take care of their parents or losing them. Just like when I lost my Dad Pete in my early 30s, to watch your peers lose their parents, and the people you love lose someone they love, it makes you feel helpless and it's heartbreaking.

The older I get, the more I study, and the more death and loss I've encountered, I've noticed something: not everyone grieves the same way. I've learned something even more epic: that how people grieve is just right for them, and that's okay! There's no right or wrong way.

Some people don't cry like I cry. Some don't feel grief the way I feel it. Some people don't see grief or perceive it how I do. I know some people who will do anything to avoid crying because, to them, tears mean weakness. They refuse to feel vulnerable, and that too is okay!

We all have to learn to survive grief. It's neither right nor wrong. I've noticed that some people, like me, cry when they need to, while others can't or won't. For some, tears are safe and okay. For others, tears are a sign of weakness.

But as I've gotten older and life has piled on more responsibilities, I've noticed something else. I've started pushing my tears aside. I'm too busy. I'm too tired. It's "not the right moment" to cry, and my mind says: Ain't nobody got time to cry.

My motto is, "If you are in the middle of a war, you don't have time to cry." Sometimes, that's true, and if I'm honest, sometimes I just don't want to feel the pain that comes with those tears, so I swallow them back down. Crying sometimes can feel exhausting.

Through Scripture, and especially through my training as a Certified Grief Educator and Coach, I've learned just how important crying really is. I find myself now literally scheduling moments just to cry. Sometimes not even for a specific reason. Sometimes my soul just needs to cry because of the weight I carry.

If I sit long enough in prayer, sometimes the tears just come without my consent or permission, and I'm like, "Wow, I guess I had some stuff in me that needed to come out."

I came across a post from an IG account, @goodneuroscience, that stopped me in my tracks:

"Crying is more than an emotional release, it's a powerful biological process that helps your body heal. Holding back tears can prolong stress, while allowing yourself to cry supports nervous system balance and mental clarity. Recognizing crying as a healing mechanism can change how we respond to our emotions, promoting resilience and recovery."

Wow. Isn't that powerful! Crying is literally part of how God designed our bodies to heal.

Then, there's Scripture. The Bible says that heaven collects our tears. Let that sink in for a second. Our tears are so precious to God that He records every single one of them and collects them in a bottle. That means every time you cry, heaven notices, and rushes in to collect your tears.

Heaven is collecting your tears! How profound and beautiful is that!

Years later, when I became a mom, I faced a moment that tested this belief. When I lost my Uncle David, my daughter was very young. I had just told her he had transitioned, and I felt a wave of emotion rise up in me.

I had a choice: Do I hold it in and cry later, or do I let her see me cry? I chose to cry in front of her.

Years prior, I would have been stoic and strong. After all, I'm Mommy and I have to demonstrate what it looks like to be strong no matter what. I cried because I needed her to know that tears are okay. I wanted her to understand that crying is a normal, healthy response when someone dies.

I didn't need to appear strong. Tears don't make me weak. In fact, tears are healing. They release pain and prevent it from getting stuck in our bodies. I learned that the hard way, by holding it in until it made me physically sick.

I needed to give her a safe space that it's okay to feel, cry, just be, and you know what? We cried together! It helped us bond, heal in connection, but also grieve in a safe space. So right now, as you read this, I'm sitting with you. If you need to cry, I'm here. No judgment.

God is here too with His bottle in hand. Your tears are valuable to God. He promises that every tear you've cried will be collected and one day will water the garden of your healing, moment by moment, millisecond by millisecond, while He is healing your land.

I love you and I'm thinking about you.

With love,
Ke'Shawn

SCRIPTURE

"You keep track of all my sorrows. You have collected all my tears in Your bottle. You have recorded each one in Your book" (**Psalm 56:8, NLT**).

REFLECTION

You don't have to hold back your tears. Crying doesn't make you weak, it's your body's way of releasing pain. In fact, letting the tears flow makes you stronger because you're allowing your heart and nervous system to heal. Pour out your heart and tears to Him. It's a safe space. He's right there, ready and waiting to meet you where you are.

REFLECTION QUESTIONS

- How do you express your pain? In what ways do you hold back your tears?
- What pain are you avoiding by not crying?
- How can you create safe moments to allow your tears to flow?
- How can you change your perspective on what crying really means?

PRAYER

Father, in the name of Jesus, I come to You right now. Sometimes I cry all the time and feel ashamed. Sometimes I want to cry, but I can't. I want to release the tears, but I don't want to feel the emotions tied to them.

I don't want to appear weak, and often, I don't make space for it because it feels too overwhelming. I pray for a holy release that I can pour all my tears into You right now, and as I cry, Your healing power will rest upon me. Every tear I shed will bring me closer and closer to healing and one step nearer to wholeness in this deep pain I carry.

Thank You for collecting every tear and holding me through every cry.

In Jesus' mighty name, Amen.

DAY 12
JOURNAL

_____
_____
_____
_____
_____
_____
_____
_____
_____
_____
_____
_____
_____
_____
_____
_____
_____
_____
_____
_____
_____
_____
_____
_____

Don't Judge My Grief

I remember getting to a place when it felt like my whole world was collapsing. I was in my 40s, had been married for a while, raising two daughters, and enduring some deeply traumatic deaths during that season. I made the decision to go to therapy.

During that time, what kept coming up in my emotions again and again was the loss of my grandmother. Although it had been many decades since she passed, I had been carrying so much grief about her for so long. I cannot tell you why, at that age and in that season, grief hit me like a flood regarding that loss.

I was only seven when she died, and the truth is, I never properly grieved that loss. I felt it, I agonized over it, but I never processed it, and there is a difference. At that very first session, my therapist asked me how I was doing. Before I knew it, I just broke. It came out of nowhere, a **Grief Burst.**

A Grief Burst is a sudden, overwhelming wave of grief that comes without warning. You do not feel it building, you do not see it coming, it just hits like a tsunami. I went to answer her and I just sobbed. OMG, that is a terrible first impression! I cried uncontrollably. I had been holding that kind of pain in for four decades, and everything in me finally erupted.

To someone on the outside, it might have seemed strange, an adult crying over a loved one lost decades ago, a grandmother at that, sobbing as if it happened yesterday. After I stopped crying, I told my therapist, "I've really been grieving my grandmother really strongly lately. It's not normal for me to cry like this, but I've been in real pain lately."

Years later, while searching for insurance paperwork online, I happened to see my therapist's notes on our first session. If I was surprised at our first encounter, she too was surprised. She wrote that it struck her as odd how I cried like I had just lost my grandmother recently and how I had poor coping skills.

I was dumbfounded to read that, and in that moment, it felt like, even in therapy, there was a quiet judgment. I was disappointed that my grief was interpreted like that. However, even therapists are human and prone to judgment. I am still the biggest advocate of therapy, but I understand they are human, just like me, and can make snap judgments.

That is called **Disenfranchised Grief.**

Disenfranchised Grief is a type of grief that people judge and do not understand because they cannot see it or do not understand it. For a while, that judgment disturbed me. OMG, me, poor coping skills! NOT! It was not until I became educated and began to truly understand why I cried like that.

This is why becoming educated on grief is so important, because sometimes, the judgment is real and people just do not understand. Now that I am educated, it was perfectly normal that I burst like that.

Here is what I understand now: If you do not emotionally process pain or trauma when it happens, your body holds on to it. It does not get old. It does not magically fade away. It feels just as raw as the moment it happened, because emotionally, you are still there.

My grandmother co-parented with my mom to help raise me. So when she died, I did not just lose a grandmother, I lost a mom, and because I never processed it, I remained that little seven-year-old girl inside, still needing to grieve her second mother figure.

As I write this, I am thinking about those of you sitting in grief right now, over someone who passed long ago, and maybe those emotions still feel as raw as the day they died.

I want you to know, it is okay. There will never be a time when you will not feel something when you think about that loss, and if anyone ever tells you:

- "You are not over that yet?"
- "You should be further along by now."
- "Wow, they are still really sad about that still?"
- "That happened so long ago, they are still sad?"
- Or, "Oh, she just lost her grandmother, I lost my mother and I am not grieving like that!"

They judge that person's significance in your life no matter what role they played, big or small. Do not believe it. Do not fall for the okey-doke. People judge grief and it feels cruel, insensitive, and wrong. You would be surprised at the stories I have heard from grievers, things people have said that were just cruel.

Do not let anyone push you along in your grieving process. Your feelings are yours. Your grief is yours. Your feelings are valid.

Your body and your soul process grief at their own pace. Do not let anyone invalidate your relationships either. Grief has no timeline. Grief is not linear, and it can last longer than anyone would expect. It is not about where others think you should be, it is about where and when your soul is ready to release it.

Sometimes, we even judge ourselves. We think we should be further along by now. But the truth is, you cannot push yourself to heal faster than your heart and soul are ready. We each find meaning and acceptance in our own time, in our own way.

So today, I encourage you:

- Be compassionate with yourself and your grief journey.
- Do not let anyone tell you where you should be.
- Do not allow anyone to minimize your feelings
- You are the only expert on your grief journey.

Your body and your soul know exactly what to do, and it will happen in its perfect time.

I have also learned this: grief does not magically go away. It will stay with you as long as you love your loved one.

But there is something called **Grief Work.** Grief Work is the intentional effort we put into processing our loss and moving toward healing. Time alone does not heal grief. It is the work we do to feel it, process it, and release it that leads to healing.

I did not know that when I was younger. My family definitely did not know about grief work either. They were trying to survive, and you do not know what you do not know.

As a matter of fact, most people have no clue that we are not helpless in grief, that there are things we can do to help ourselves heal. That was groundbreaking to know in my 40s, there are things I can do to help myself process grief.

But now, as a Certified Grief Coach and Educator, I understand it and find ways to help myself and others process it. I love you, and I want you to know where you are is okay. Your grief is okay, and in the perfect time, as you embrace and intentionally step into your healing journey, you will move forward.

Next time someone has something to say about how you are grieving, politely tell them:

"Do not judge my grief! Allow me space and time to process at my pace and space. Support me where you can, and pray for me where you are concerned."

I love you and I am thinking about you.

With love,
Ke'Shawn

SCRIPTURE

"Precious in the sight of The Lord is the death of His saints" (**Psalm 116:15, NKJV**).

REFLECTION

Even The Lord grieves. It makes Him sad to see the death of His loved ones. If the Creator of the universe understands the sadness of death, that's all the approval you need.

He gets it. He understands. He knows, and He is with you.

Death in His sight is holy, sacred, and He rejoices to be with us again. But also, He understands the fragility of that death and what it costs us on earth. For Him, it's both sacred, sorrowful, and celebratory, precious and delicate in His sight.

No one can walk this road with you, and no one is capable of holding your pain. Take your time. You are your own expert, and no one has the right to tell you how far along you should be.

REFLECTION QUESTIONS

- In what ways has your grief been judged by others or even by yourself?
- Have you ever cried over someone who passed long ago, but it felt like yesterday?
- How can you honor those feelings instead of judging them?
- How can you advocate for yourself when others try to invalidate your grief?

PRAYER

Lord, I come to You with a humble, grieving heart. Help me focus on You when I feel alone and misunderstood. Help me remember that You understand my grief even when the world judges it. Give me a deep, inner knowing that I am exactly where I need to be. If I'm not, show me gently how to move toward healing.

You don't judge me. You don't shame me for where I am. You don't demand I move before I'm ready. You gently guide me toward healing.

I forgive others for judging what they don't understand. I thank You for Your undying and unconditional love, to meet and accept me exactly where I am.

I love and thank You,

In Jesus' mighty name, Amen.

DAY 13
JOURNAL

Faith Over Fear

Sudden death can bring on all sorts of fears. One moment everything is fine, and the next, your whole life changes.

Fears Grow in Grief! Common fears include forgetting your loved one, grieving too long, breaking down in public, feeling like the pain will never end, or fearing the future. These fears are normal and deserve compassion.

Your body remembers. Your mind remembers it too. After that moment, your body starts bracing for similar moments. Every time the phone rings, especially late at night. Every time someone sounds panicky when they say, "I need to tell you something."

You stay in **fight-or-flight mode** because you don't know, moment by moment, what's coming next. Who's going to die? What's the next worst thing that's about to happen? Fight-or-flight is when your body stays on high alert, preparing to protect you from real or perceived danger.

Grief disorients you. You feel unstable, like you can't find your footing or a secure place to stand. Like at any moment you're going to get knocked over.

Having **cumulative loss** in my life, I never fully learned to enjoy happy moments. They were always short-lived. I didn't realize that until I got married. My husband pointed it out. He noticed that something great would happen, and I'd be excited for a moment, but my excitement would quickly turn into worry or fear.

After going through training, becoming certified, and learning more about mental health and grief, I finally realized something: No, I'm not crazy for not being able to remain joyful for long periods of time without going into worry. No, I'm not trying to be miserable or be a worrywart.

He never said that, but I started thinking that when I began to get curious why my joy was short-lived. One day God revealed it to me, and it was highlighted again during my grief trainings.

My brain had been hard-wired to protect me from danger from moment to moment. Because of cumulative loss, I was always prepared and ready for the next catastrophic thing. I was always in fight-or-flight, bracing for the next big loss. Traumatized by death, my **nervous system** got stuck, constantly preparing for a catastrophe.

Your **sympathetic nervous system** activates fight-or-flight, releasing cortisol and adrenaline to protect you from danger. Think of it as the **body's alarm system**, alerting your brain (mainly the **amygdala**, the emotional center, and the **prefrontal cortex**, the decision-making center) that something scary or dangerous is happening. It gets your heart racing, your muscles ready, your senses sharper, all to help you survive.

But when trauma and grief happen again and again, your **Parasympathetic Nervous System**, the part that calms you down, can shut down. This system is like the body's brake pedal. It helps slow your heart rate, calm your breathing, and signal to your brain that it's safe to relax. It works closely with the parts of the brain that help you rest, recover, and feel safe.

I didn't understand this until I sat under **Alex Howard's** *Reset Your Nervous System program*. That's when I finally saw the connection. My nervous system was out of balance because of years of sudden, cumulative loss. When death can occur at any moment, it makes life unstable and hard to adjust, and that's completely outside of our control.

It was at that moment that I had to lean fully into my faith. For most of my life, I felt like the bottom was about to fall out at any moment, and I braced myself as if it would. But now, I understand this:

As long as Jesus is in the boat with me, the boat will not capsize. It will not flip over, and I will not fall out. Even if the worst thing happens, I can take comfort knowing Jesus is with me. While the storm rages, He is still in the boat, and as long as He's there, we will not sink.

I know grief has traumatized you. I know that phone call, that day, that moment that everything changed, it rewired you too. Your nervous system feels like it can't handle one more thing. I understand. I've been there.

So today, I want to sit with you and remind you: As long as Jesus is in your boat, and as long as He's in mine, we're going to be okay. The boat will not capsize and we will not drown.

We can trust Him, moment by moment, second by second, millisecond by millisecond. He will never let us go. God's got us, and together, we're walking this faith journey, knowing that no matter what comes, He is with us. He will not let us fail or fall.

I love you and I'm thinking about you.

With love,
Ke'Shawn

SCRIPTURE

"He got up, rebuked the wind and said to the waves, 'Quiet! Be still!' Then the wind died down and it was completely calm" (**Mark 4:39, NIV**).

"You make me sure-footed like a deer; You set me secure on the heights" (**Psalm 18:33, NIV**).

REFLECTION

Jesus was in the boat while the winds and waves beat against it, yet He said, "Peace, be still." Even when life feels like it's spinning out of control, He's still in the boat with you, bringing peace to your storm. Just call out His name. He will quiet your storm.

REFLECTION QUESTIONS

- What fears come up for you in grief?
- How can you check in with yourself, moment by moment, to move from fight-or-flight to calm and healing?
- How can you care for yourself when fear and anxiety rise up?
- How can you help yourself in the midst of a crisis?

PRAYER

Heavenly Father,

I thank You for this day. I thank You that You are sovereign over my life and every detail of my journey. In the name of Jesus, You stand with me, before me, and all around me.

You speak over every storm: "Peace, be still."

I speak Your peace over everything that concerns me, over my family, my loved ones, and the pain of my loss.

Father, I pray that You restore what trauma has damaged in my mind and heart. Reset my nervous system. Regulate what has been stuck in fight-or-flight. Cut every soul tie to past catastrophes and imagined fears that keep me bound.

I speak to my mind and my heart:

Peace, be still.

Waves, be quiet.

Winds, be calm.

I receive Your perfect peace. You make me sure-footed like a deer; I shall not be moved. Let shalom be my portion in the land of the living. Let Your peace and rest settle over me right now.

In Jesus' mighty name, Amen.

DAY 14
JOURNAL

_____

_____

_____

_____

_____

_____

_____

_____

_____

_____

_____

_____

_____

_____

_____

_____

_____

_____

_____

_____

_____

_____

_____

_____

— DAY 15 —

When Life Feels Unfair, Remember My Son

ave you ever looked at the pain in the world and thought, "God, where are You? Why aren't You doing something? Why aren't You moving and showing Yourself strong? Why aren't You doing anything to stop it? You're God, You can stop it!"

The COVID-19 pandemic hit New Rochelle, New York, before anywhere else in the United States. I live in New Rochelle, and it was one of the scariest moments of our lives outside of 9/11. The National Guard came. People were dying by the thousands. Streets were barricaded. Stores were closed. Everything was shut down, and we were scared to death. Every trip out of the house with my husband felt like stepping into the Twilight Zone.

We were afraid to touch anything, afraid to even move. Real talk, we were scared to death! I've never in my lifetime experienced anything like it. I remember playing Kari Jobe's song "The Blessing" because it spoke of the goodness of God. I also remember sitting on my terrace, looking at the world all around me, praying, yet feeling utterly despondent.

With the world shutting down, with deaths all around me, and with tragedy piling up day after day, I sat before The Lord and said: "There are people dying everywhere. There's war, murder, sex trafficking, children suffering; the most horrific things imaginable. You sit by and let it happen. You're allowing people to die by the thousands, millions worldwide. Where are You?

I'm singing of Your goodness, but right now, You don't feel very good. How can You allow these things to happen, especially to innocent children? You see this, why aren't You stopping it?" For days, I prayed that, and for days, The Lord was silent. Then one quiet morning, I felt Him speak to my heart:

"When you see these horrific things happen: innocent lives treacherously destroyed by violence, good people taken too soon, diseases, epidemics, pandemics, you think I'm unfair. I want you to reflect and remember My Son. Yeshua. Emmanuel. Jesus the Christ, the Savior of the world, My only begotten Son, was not exempt from torture, humiliation, rejection, grief, despair, and death so brutal that He became unrecognizable.

If that happened to the Son of God, do you think you will never face suffering? The truth is, unfair and terrible things do happen to really great people. You live in a fallen world where the enemy is real. His goal is to destroy you and all that I created. Sin entered through Adam and Eve, and because of that, the world is prone to brokenness and pain.

When you cannot see My hand move, and evil seems to prevail, trust My face. Trust My character. If my Son was not spared the sufferings of this world, neither will My people be, as I accomplish My ultimate purpose in their lives. My ways are not your ways, and My thoughts are not your thoughts. Yet, I have good plans for you, plans for hope and a future. Even when evil happens, My heart toward you is good. I'm not asking you to pretend you're okay when life feels unbearable. I'm asking you to trust Me when you don't understand, and when you can't see My hand, look at My face."

When The Lord spoke that to me, there was nothing left to say. I pray that what you just read may not "fix" everything, but may quiet your soul and bring peace in the middle of your storm. I know we sit here together with the same questions, feelings of rage, and sometimes anger at the sufferings of this world, at a senseless, tragic loss and inhuman suffering.

I will never try to Brightside you, to put a positive spin on your loss and slap a scripture on it. I don't know what happened to someone you love, and for that, my heart is so heavy and sorrowful for your loss and what you've endured.

It'll take time for this revelation to settle in, I understand, and especially, The Lord understands. Take your time. It's okay. You'll never be "okay" with tragedy; you'll never find meaning in it either.

It is my prayer that you find comfort in knowing that His Son wasn't spared, and God Himself, as Abba Father, has felt what you feel. He went through it too. God sits with you in your heartbreak. He knows exactly how you feel– a beautiful life gone too soon, senseless and tragic–and is fully able to carry the sorrow with you. May He speak to you right now and give you peace.

I love you and I'm thinking about you.

With love,
Ke'Shawn

SCRIPTURE

"For My thoughts are not your thoughts, neither are your ways My ways...As the heavens are higher than the earth, so are My ways higher than your ways and My thoughts than your thoughts" (**Isaiah 55:8–9, NIV**).

"For I know the plans I have for you," declares The Lord, "plans to prosper you and not to harm you, plans to give you hope and a future" (**Jeremiah 29:11, NIV**).

"After you have suffered a little while, God Himself will restore you and make you strong, firm and steadfast" (**1 Peter 5:10, NIV**).

"For God so loved the world that He gave His only be-gotten Son, that whoever believes in Him shall not perish but have everlasting life" (**John 3:16, NIV**).

REFLECTION

We may never fully understand what The Lord is doing. But over the years, I've learned this: He wants us to trust Him.

That may feel impossible when the pain is raw and unfair, but healing doesn't come all at once. It's a moment-by-moment decision to take His hand and let His grace hold you. Even when life feels unbearably unfair, remember, God's Son suffered too, and Abba Father suffered as a parent.

If He did not abandon Jesus on the cross, He will not abandon you now. He knows. He understands. He sits with you now.

REFLECTION QUESTIONS

- What questions do you wrestle with when it comes to God and suffering?
- How does knowing Jesus suffered unfairly shift your perspective on tragedy?
- How can you lean into faith when your loss feels unbearably unfair?
- How can the revelation of God being Abba Father, a parent losing His Son, help you with your grief process?

PRAYER

Father, in the name of Jesus, I come to You broken, confused, and grieving. I've lost someone I love, and I lost them too soon. Supernaturally give me the peace I need to take even one step toward healing.

Help me bring my real feelings to You, even when I think You're unfair, even when it feels like You're not good. Teach me to come to You raw and honest, because You can handle my honesty. Give me boldness to approach Your throne, and grace to find comfort and peace in my time of need.

Thank You for hearing me and for never letting me go.

In Jesus' mighty name, Amen.

DAY 15
JOURNAL

_____

_____

_____

_____

_____

_____

_____

_____

_____

_____

_____

_____

_____

_____

_____

_____

_____

_____

_____

_____

_____

_____

_____

_____

Grief Is Love

W hen I started my business as a Grief Coach and Educator, I had to figure out what I was going to do with all this training and real-life experience. I was blessed with a team of people, my SCORE business mentor and his colleague, who helped me with the task of putting together my website.

The web expert told me that I really needed to put a headline at the top that would grab readers as soon as they landed on the site. I researched and then one day, I asked my mom, "When you think of the word grief, what comes to mind?"

Her answer to me was, "It's a terrible thing. It's a terrible, terrible thing."

I agreed with her sentiments 100%. For all of my life, I felt the same way. Grief was dark. It was heavy. It was a terrible, terrible thing, something to be avoided at all costs.

But that changed for me. After decades of feeling the same way, during the very first week of my grief coaching certification course, I discovered that while it's common for people to see grief this way, at its core, grief is really the expression of love. We grieve because we love, and because we lost what we loved.

The definition of **Grief** is a change that you never wanted to happen; it is the loss of something or someone you love. You can't grieve something you don't love. So when you find yourself grieving, what you're experiencing is you loving them. But now, in this new space and time, you're really missing them and longing for them. Understanding that one principle changed everything for me. It shifted how I approached my entire grieving process.

So, I sit with you right now in this valley of grief, knowing that it is heavy. It feels dark, lonely, and it is a road that only you and God can truly take.

No one can go through it with you, even if they can relate to the loss or even knew your loved one. But if we can look at grief through a new lens and see it as the love that connects us to the person we lost, grief becomes the bond that still binds us. It's the ache of missing them, the pain of not wanting them to leave, but it's all wrapped up in love. I pray this one simple concept transforms how you view grief; that it's not something to be avoided.

When you feel grief, you're loving and missing your person, so let it flow! Don't shove it down or push it aside. Your heart is longing for and loving them in that moment. Grief will forever be a part of your life story, woven into the moments of your life. It is a companion, and it is my prayer that God will give us the grace, the strength, the knowledge, and the understanding to embrace this forever companion called Grief.

To know grief is to know love. I love you, and I sit in grief with you while we sojourn, explore, embrace, and navigate this new love together.

I love you and I'm thinking about you.

With love,
Ke'Shawn

SCRIPTURE

"For God so loved the world that He gave His only begotten Son, that whoever believes in Him shall not perish but have everlasting life" **(John 3:16, NKJV).**

REFLECTION

We have yet to fully tap into what true love looks like. Love isn't always simple, it's complex, sometimes hurtful, and it doesn't always feel pretty. God loved us so much that He sacrificed His greatest love through pain and suffering.

Love always costs us something. We grieve because we love and because we dared to love fully, allowing that love to transform us. Now we hurt because the love we want close and near feels far away.

But as long as you carry that love, they live on in you. That love is forever the stronghold that binds you, and it is a gift from God.

REFLECTION QUESTIONS

- In what ways can you embrace grief as love?
- How can you allow grief space in your life?
- How can knowing that grief is truly love transform your life?

PRAYER

Father God, in the name of Jesus, I pray for Your love to flow through me like a gentle river right now. I pray that You allow my mind and my heart to be open to what true love looks like even when it doesn't feel pretty, even when it hurts, and especially through loss.

Help me embrace this new season of experiencing love in the form of grief. Transform me through it, leading me to new purpose and new meaning. I pray that my grief, expressed as love, is not in vain, that it will birth a harvest that spreads the love I feel for my loved one to the people around me.

Allow my grief to transform me and be used for Your glory.

In Jesus' mighty name, Amen.

DAY 16
JOURNAL

_____
_____
_____
_____
_____
_____
_____
_____
_____
_____
_____
_____
_____
_____
_____
_____
_____
_____
_____
_____
_____
_____
_____
_____

I Miss You

Sometimes grief hits like waves. Sometimes you can be focused on the moment, going about your day, not even thinking about your loved one, and then suddenly something you see, hear, or smell in the air overwhelms you and floods your mind with all of the feelings.

One day I was looking out the window, the same window I look out of every night, and it never seemed to bother me. But this particular day, I looked to the right of my window and saw the bus stop my grandmother used to bring me to when I was a little girl. I've sat there, looking out this same window thousands of times, and never thought about it.

But this one particular day, I thought about all the times she walked me to the bus, how she stood with me waiting for the bus to come. Every single time the bus would pull up, I'd be scared to death because I didn't want to leave her.

It was like I was going to school for the first time every single day. I reacted the same way every time. I didn't like leaving her and wasn't that fond of trading my time with her for going to school. I don't know why, but very day, as I went off to kindergarten, I was afraid she wouldn't pick me up. Yet, every day, she showed up.

Every single day, she walked into that kindergarten class like an angel, and would light up my world. It was like I was seeing her for the very first time. Outside of my mother, who is my angel, right next to her, my grandmother was "Mommy" too. She was absolutely my bestest friend.

Sometimes people underestimate our relationships. Just because she was a grandmother doesn't mean she was "just a grandmother." She was a mother. So when I lost her, I lost a second mother, and my heart couldn't differentiate anything else. I lost a mom.

People often judge our relationships, and it's hurtful because they minimize not just the relationship but also the pain and how it impacted us. She stood right there alongside my mom, along with my grandfather, and helped raise my sister and me. So, looking at that street corner, all the memories came flooding in, and at that moment, what came to my mind was:

"Ain't nobody got time to cry."

That's how I coped with grief for decades. I just shoved it down, pushing it aside because I didn't have time. I didn't want to feel, and I didn't want to be in that moment. It was too much to handle.

But my body and my soul, in their perfect wisdom, said no. They told me it was okay to miss her. The tears came without my permission. They just flooded, and I sobbed because in that moment. I remembered, and I missed her desperately.

I miss all of our moments. I especially miss those mornings of her putting me on the bus and picking me up from school.

I know right now your heart is longing for your loved one too. Whether your loss was yesterday, a few days ago, months ago, years or even decades ago, it's painful. It truly hurts. I sit with you as you miss your love too.

Together, today, as I'm writing this, my heart hurts, and as you're reading this, I know your heart hurts too. Let's embrace this moment of missing our loved one. It's okay. It's safe to feel.

You're not doing it alone. I'm sitting right here with my achy heart too. Let's pause, breathe, and whisper:

"I miss you, I miss you, I miss you! I wish you were here. I remember when... I miss the most... Thank You for... I'm grateful for..."

The ache of longing can sometimes bring you to your knees. It's an unbearable pain, like a cruel animal trap with sharp teeth ripping your heart apart. I'm so sorry that when you're missing them, you feel that pain too. It hurts so bad.

I'm sorry your heart is aching right now. Mine is too. It hurts so badly. So let's sit together, remember, and process the pain together. As I process my pain, I'm thinking about you too.

I love you, and please know that you are not alone.

With love,
Ke'Shawn

SCRIPTURE

"We don't grieve as the world grieves, for we will all be caught up to meet our loved ones in the air" (**1 Thessalonians 4:13–17, NKJV**).

"The God of all comfort will comfort you" (**2 Corinthians 1:3–4, NKJV**).

REFLECTION

As a Christian, I've learned over the years to embrace the longing instead of shoving it down. What has brought me comfort is knowing this separation is not forever. I miss them right now, and only God can comfort me in this moment, but the assurance that it's not goodbye, it's "I'll see you later," gives me peace.

It's not forever, and that brings comfort because what was can be again. It doesn't take away the pain, but it sure does give me something to look forward to: that I'll see them again. That brings me comfort and peace. It's not over. But in the meantime, it's okay to long and miss them. Let it flow. This moment will pass. I promise you.

REFLECTION QUESTIONS

- Who are you missing right now?
- What memories come up as you're missing them?
- What can you do to comfort yourself in this moment?
- How can you embrace processing the pain you feel when you miss your loved one?

PRAYER

Father God, in the name of Jesus, comfort my aching heart as I long for my loved one. There's no other pain in the world like this, to miss someone and no longer have access to them here. I want to feel them. I want to hear their voice. I miss their hugs. I miss their touch.

That's the part that feels like it kills me on the inside. I know You've said we will be together again, but sometimes that doesn't help me in the moment when my heart is breaking. Only You can comfort me in a way that silences my anxiety and my separation until the time comes for us to be together again.

Help me find meaning and purpose in this moment until that day comes. It is my prayer that one day I will remember them with love and less pain.

In Jesus' mighty name, Amen.

DAY 17
JOURNAL

_____

_____

_____

_____

_____

_____

_____

_____

_____

_____

_____

_____

_____

_____

_____

_____

_____

_____

_____

_____

_____

_____

_____

_____

— DAY 18 —

A New Anticipated Future

*H*ave you ever daydreamed about your future, what it would look like, what you hoped it would be?

Most girls dream and long for the day they get married. We have an **anticipated trajectory**. This is the picture of what life will look like, the dream, the plan, the story we expect to live out. But life happens, and what we sometimes hope for, the dream we pictured, doesn't turn out the way we expected.

That's grief!

The Bible talks about how "hope deferred makes the heart sick" (Proverbs 13:12). You're waiting and waiting for something to happen. Your soul feels sick because you've been waiting so long, and then life hits hard, and disappointment shakes your heart. This is especially true with death.

You had a vision for your life, for your family, for your loved one and when their life is taken, your heart has to make an impossible adjustment. The future you dreamed of will never look the same without them in it. That's a dream crushed. That's one of the hardest, most disappointing parts of grief.

All the **Secondary Losses**; not just mourning the death, but now grieving over all the changes that happened or no longer happened because of that death. Secondary losses are all the ripple effects of grief. The layers of loss that follow after the first. It's missing their voice on the other end of the phone, their presence at birthdays and holidays, their role in the family, the security they gave, the plans you made together, and the future you thought was certain.

It's not just one loss. It's loss upon loss, all tied back to the person you loved. All the adjustments you're forced to make, because they can't be part of the future you were building together. Now you're facing **anticipated reality**. This is when what you hoped for is no longer your reality.

Your reality now is that your loved one died, and they won't be there for the vision you held for so long. When we lose someone we love deeply, everything about our future shifts. The wedding we imagined. The children we dreamed of raising. The vacations we thought we'd take. The home we planned to build. All the family moments we longed for. Shattered.

All of it, instantly gone. We not only grieve the person we've lost, we grieve the future we'll never have with them. That loss cuts deep because it feels like our whole life has been rewritten without our permission.

I remember after my dad, Pete, passed. He was supposed to walk me down the aisle with my biological father. That was the vision. That was always the plan. But when he suddenly passed, everything changed.

It changed the path my now-husband and I were on. It changed the relationship they were building. It changed the tux fittings. It changed how I imagined my wedding day, and it changed how my mom and I had to think about our future without him.

It was supposed to be both of my dads, my biological father and Pete, but now, Pete was no longer here. I had a choice. I had to do everything without him or find ways to incorporate him. I refused to let his memory and presence be lost just because he wasn't physically there.

Instead of my dad walking me down the aisle alone, my mom and my dad walked with me. I chose to create space for him at the wedding too. We had a pew reserved in his honor with the best view in the church. We had a table with rose petals and his picture greeting everyone who walked in.

For my vow renewal, I even designed a table, refurbished from a wooden spool, to honor him because he was always refurbishing furniture. He had a place at my vow renewal.

This is what's called a **new anticipated trajectory.** It's where you take what was supposed to be and merge it with what is, creating a new future that still carries your loved one with you. It's about acceptance and finding meaning wrapped into one.

Did I like that he wasn't physically there? Absolutely not. I hated it. But I had to accept what was, and in that acceptance, I had to figure out, "How do I merge him into this new future I'm building without him here?"

Even in the midst of this loss, I was truly grateful and had to lean into gratitude. Although Pete was no longer with us, I was blessed by my biological dad being a strong tower. I was grateful for his presence in my life and for sharing in that moment, along with my mother as well. That too was a dream come true.

That's where meaning began to unfold. Even with a

broken heart in hand, I've learned that God can take what's shattered and merge the broken pieces with His potential for healing.

Is it easy? No. It's earth-shattering for your soul. You didn't want this life, but now you're here. So now what? I hold onto this truth: "He gives us beauty for ashes" (Isaiah 61:3).

I know this isn't the way you wanted beauty to resurrect in your life. But to preserve their **legacy**, to keep their love alive, we each have to learn to honor them and bring them with us into our new future.

That part of the grief journey takes time. Every thought of them is painful at first, especially when you long for something new but feel trapped by grief. But one thing I know: God is with you. He will not abandon you in this transition. One millisecond at a time, He will give you strength and grace to create new stories, new chapters, new moments, and in those moments you get to take your loved one with you.

As long as you hold them dear in your heart, as long as you remember the beautiful times you shared, you carry the gift of God. Hold the love you had together, and they absolutely get to be a part of your new life.

I'm sending you so much love in the middle of your disappointment. May the grace of God comfort your aching heart, fill your void, and guide you, one millisecond at a time, as He shows you how to move forward with Him.

I love you and I'm thinking about you.

With love,
Ke'Shawn

SCRIPTURE

"For I know the plans I have for you," declares the Lord, "plans to prosper you and not to harm you, plans to give you hope and a future" **(Jeremiah 29:11, NIV).**

"Trust in the Lord with all your heart and lean not on your own understanding; in all your ways submit to Him, and He will make your paths straight" **(Proverbs 3:5–6, NIV).**

REFLECTION

God knows what we can't yet see. Even as we grieve the future we longed for, He has a way of weaving beauty into the broken pieces. It's okay to cry out over what you've lost.

It's okay to wonder how this story could ever be good.

But little by little, God plants seeds of hope in the soil of shattered dreams. One day, those seeds will bloom into a future only He could imagine.

REFLECTION QUESTIONS

- What future did you imagine with your loved one that now feels lost?
- How has grief changed the trajectory of your life story?
- What small ways can you invite God to lead you into a new future you didn't anticipate?

PRAYER

Father God, I am heartbroken over the future I dreamed of that will never be. I never imagined living without my loved one. I don't know how to picture life moving forward without them by my side. Give me strength for this unwanted new anticipated future.

Help me trust that even when I can't see how this story unfolds. You see it all. Lead me gently into each new day, and when I feel crushed under the weight of "what could've been."

Remind me that You still have good plans for me. I give You my broken dreams and ask You to hold my heart as You write the next chapter of my life.

In Jesus' mighty name, Amen.

DAY 18
JOURNAL

_____

_____

_____

_____

_____

_____

_____

_____

_____

_____

_____

_____

_____

_____

_____

_____

_____

_____

_____

_____

_____

— DAY 19 —

The River of Grief

*H*ealing takes time. I know, I know, you're over it already. Me too!

Have you ever wanted to be further along in your grief, and felt impatient with the process? You're already "over it," but grief has a say-so too! You take two steps forward, and BAM! Two steps back!

Grief is like a river, always flowing, changing, or shifting. As nature would have it, some kids come by and throw a pebble in it, and it ripples. A bird flies overhead and drops a big branch into the water while building its nest. A fisherman speeds by in his boat, sending waves crashing to the banks.

That river is constantly subjected to changes around it, and as much as it longs for still waters, disturbances happen: disruptions, floods, storms, man-made intrusions. Anything can cause catastrophic shifts.

Grief is no different. It takes everything in you just to keep your head above water when you're grieving. Some days, it takes every ounce of energy just to get out of bed, go to the bathroom, or do anything at all– especially when you have to return to work while still shattered inside.

You're spinning, numb, suffering from **Grief Brain**.

Grief Brain is when your brain and nervous system are literally on overwhelm. Your reasoning, executive function, and working memory are clouded, leaving you stuck in a daze, unable to figure out the next moment or decision. Sometimes you're praying that no one says anything careless to you, because your nervous system is on edge, and you can't take one more thing. Your **Neuroception,** your subconscious ability to detect safety or danger without conscious thought, is scanning for cues that put you into fight-or-flight survival mode.

That survival mode might look like:

- **Fight** – feeling irritable, defensive, or ready to argue to protect yourself.
- **Flight** – wanting to run away or escape situations that feel overwhelming.
- **Freeze** – shutting down, feeling numb, unable to move or think.
- **Fawn** – trying to appease others to feel safe, even while neglecting your own needs.

Sometimes, it's a complete shutdown where you can't process anything at all. If you find yourself here, you are not alone, and it's okay. Like a river, one small disturbance can send waves crashing and turbulence swirling, sometimes knocking you completely off your feet. But Jesus...

Jesus is a soft place to land. Take His hand and don't let go. For now, just live one moment at a time. From second to second, you may feel multiple emotions at one time. Grief is unpredictable. You'll have no clue where you are in your emotions, let alone letting others in on how you're feeling.

If no one told you this today, I'm proud of you. What you are going through is normal, and you are doing grief really well. With everything you're facing, you're still sitting here with me, reading these words, sitting with Christ, and arming yourself with self-care. That takes courage. That's commitment.

Resilience doesn't always look like conquering the world. Sometimes it looks like learning about grief, tending to your pain, showing up to read this devotional. If all you managed to do today was brush your teeth, that's resilience. If you got out of bed, ate something, or simply breathed through another minute, that's resilience.

Expect setbacks in this process. Right now, the journey may feel erratic. After all, your life has been ripped out from under you. Expect that every moment may bring unexpected waves you can't control. But here's what you can control:

- Have a Scripture ready to ground you when turbulence hits.
- Breathe through the moment, pray, and trust Christ to hold you steady.
- Educate yourself about your grief process so you can name what you're experiencing and gather tools, like you're doing right now.
- Be patient and compassionate with yourself, just as you would be with a dear friend.

I'm proud of you. You are not alone. I'm walking alongside you in this moment, and the Great I Am is here to guide and comfort you through every wave. Hold on, one millisecond at a time. God will not let you go.

I love you, and I'm thinking about you.

With love,
Ke'Shawn

Scripture

"'Though the mountains be shaken and the hills be removed, yet My unfailing love for you will not be shaken nor My covenant of peace be removed,' says The Lord, who has compassion on you" (**Isaiah 54:10, NIV**).

Reflection

Things change. With all the changes you're facing right now, you're longing for something to stabilize. I wish I could promise you that life would suddenly feel steady again, but I can't. I know it feels like the very ground beneath you has been ripped away. But here's what will never change: God's love for you, His covenant of peace, His promise to never leave you, even as hills, mountains, and beloved people in your life are removed. The Lord will never change and will shelter you in this storm. You shall not be moved!

Reflection Questions

- In what ways has a pebble, branch, or boulder rocked your river of grief?
- How did you handle it
- What practical ways can you prepare for future moments that bring heightened emotions, so you can navigate those rough waters with Christ's help?

PRAYER

Father God, in the name of Jesus, I pray right now that You would enter my mind and heart, quiet my storm and speak shalom over me. I ask that You cancel every assignment of the enemy that comes to disturb my peace, disrupt my healing, or destroy my rest.

Lord, I confess that in this season, peace feels like a stranger. Strength feels gone. Faith feels faint. Parts of me feel dormant, dying, beyond repair. But right now, I speak life over myself.

I call on the breath of God, the wind of the Spirit, to blow through me and strengthen me on every side.

Where I feel inwardly dead, resurrect hope and joy. Where I feel weak, breathe new strength into me. Give me wisdom to care for myself during these tough moments. Teach me how to show myself the same love and patience that You freely give me and that I would extend to a dear friend.

Grant me grace to make it through just one moment, and then the next, until I make it through the day, and as the days pass, remind me: You are my unshakable joy. You are my peace, and I thank You for it.

In Jesus' mighty name, Amen.

DAY 19
JOURNAL

_____
_____
_____
_____
_____
_____
_____
_____
_____
_____
_____
_____
_____
_____
_____
_____
_____
_____
_____
_____
_____
_____
_____
_____
_____

They Just Don't Get It

o you ever feel like nobody gets it? Like they have no clue what you're feeling right now, or what you just endured? You're absolutely right, they don't!

People can empathize with you, sympathize with you, or say they've had a similar loss, but they didn't have your specific loss. Their loved one didn't die; your loved one died. Even if they did lose someone, the circumstances, events, timing, and everything considered are still different. It's never a good practice to compare grief.

But some people, in their effort to relate, try to compare their loss to yours, thinking it might comfort you where you are, and in those moments, be patient. Sometimes you will connect with someone. People will have an impact on you or connect with you in ways that truly resonate. For those moments, embrace them. They're rare and God-sent.

What happens often in grief is that sometimes our pain brings up other people's pain. While trying to connect with us, they begin to think about their own story, feeling empathy and sympathy for what we're going through. But in doing so, they sometimes overshadow our experience. It often suffocates your story, and it becomes about them.

Have you ever had that experience? You're trying to share your pain, and all of a sudden, someone begins to dominate the conversation with their feelings. It's no longer about you. I remember when my uncle was dying. I was sharing with someone who had also recently lost someone very important to them. While I was trying to share my moment, they were trying to share theirs. I found myself getting angry because I felt like I had to shove down what I was feeling just to hear them, but I was no longer being heard.

When people can't understand where you are, what you're feeling, what your needs are, or simply sit and listen, it can make you feel resentful for ever opening up. You shut down completely and decide, at that moment, you're not going to talk about it anymore.

Here's what I learned: We're all hurting. We're all trying to be seen, and sometimes, the person you need to talk to just isn't available in that moment. They are so deep in their pain that they don't have the capacity or space to sit with your pain. Don't get mad. They may not be the person to get comfort or consolation from in that moment, and that's okay.

There are several reasons why we sometimes can't connect with others in our pain. Some people, because we live in a grief-illiterate culture, simply don't know how to comfort others or sit with them in pain. This is called **Grief Illiteracy,** when people lack the understanding, awareness, and skills to respond to grief with empathy and care. The truth is, grief makes people uncomfortable.

Our grief can make people scared because they don't know what to do with it. Our grief can make people afraid because they start imagining if it happened to them. When that happens, they leave, and that part is normal. It's not helpful to you at that moment, but it is normal.

The best thing you can do is understand that there will be people with whom you can share, and people with whom you can't. Don't hold that against them. It's hard for two people to be fully seen at the same time, even while grieving the same person. Sometimes, the best thing we can do is step away, get the support we need elsewhere in a safe space, and then return to support those around us.

It's like a crisis on an airplane: put your mask on first, then your child's, so you can help them. The same goes for grief. Sometimes you won't be able to find support from those closest to you. They will not be your main source of support. So if you feel resentful because they don't get it, perhaps in this moment, they simply can't.

Understand that many people don't have **Grief Literacy.** Grief literacy means understanding what grief is and how to support yourself and others through it. It's having the knowledge and compassion to care for people who are hurting and to respond in ways that bring comfort instead of more pain. Most people are simply not equipped to serve others in grief. In those moments, you have to realize who your tribe is. Find the people who get you, where you feel comfortable, and most importantly, where you feel heard and safe.

We heal in connection. God did not intend for us to heal alone. Everything God does, He does in teams. He sends trusted advisors and counselors. God sends people to help us process, get through the moment, and love on us when we're unable to love ourselves.

I've spent a lot of time angry at people who couldn't meet me where I was. The truth is, they weren't supposed to. To truly meet you, someone would have to move beyond themselves, and some people are too blindsided to see the full picture. Even family, the closest people to you, will not always get what you're feeling.

Here's the beauty: There is a place to go, and that place is God. I know sometimes we want people in human form, and when we get those people, hallelujah, praise God! But sometimes, when God doesn't send those people, and we find ourselves utterly alone because no one gets what we're going through, He wants you to rely solely on Him because He gets it. With Him, there is no judgment.

Forgive. I know you're angry. I know you're alone. I know this is the loneliest road you'll ever have to take. But please know this: as I've come to learn, you're not walking it alone. I know it's hard to sit by yourself right now. I know it's hard to be alone. Sometimes keeping busy helps, too. But if you can take a few seconds, just stop, breathe, and receive.

Clench your fist literally, and know God is holding your fist with you. You're holding His hand together. He will not let you go.

I love you, and I'm always proud of you and thinking of you!

With love,
Ke'Shawn

SCRIPTURE

"He was despised and rejected by mankind, a man of suffering, and familiar with pain. Like one from whom people hide their faces He was despised, and we held Him in low esteem" (**Isaiah 53:3, NIV**).

REFLECTION

Jesus was the loneliest man on earth. He was the Son of God. The people He created to love rejected Him, abused Him, abandoned Him, betrayed Him, and later, killed Him. The Bible says that after He suffered a little while, The Lord received Him and exalted Him. While you're going through this dark and lonely place, know that God has not forsaken you. I know it may feel like that when you can't see His hand or His face.

Lean on and repeat every day His promises. Your faith may be shaken, but faith comes by hearing, and hearing by the Word of God. If you can listen to His Word every day, your spirit will be strengthened. It may take some time, but keep persisting.

REFLECTION QUESTIONS

- What has surprised you about grief on your journey?
- In what ways have people not understood your grief and pain?
- What do you wish people knew?
- How can you help others understand and meet you where you are, and advocate for yourself?

PRAYER

Father God, in the name of Jesus, I feel alone. I have never felt this alone in my life, and I hate this feeling. I pray, in the name of Jesus, that You overwhelm me with Your presence, so I know You are near. Your Word says You will never leave me or forsake me. Right now, I pray that You give me peace and overshadow me with Your presence.

In Jesus' mighty name, Amen.

DAY 20
JOURNAL

_____

_____

_____

_____

_____

_____

_____

_____

_____

_____

_____

_____

_____

_____

_____

_____

_____

_____

_____

_____

_____

_____

_____

_____

_____

_____

When the Walls Are Closing In:

THE IMPORTANCE OF SELF-CARE

*D*oes it feel like the four walls are closing in on you? In grief, it can feel like you're being swallowed whole. When you lose a loved one, you're often forced into Task Mode, a state where you focus on all the responsibilities of planning and handling your loved one's affairs.

Task Mode looks like this:

- Planning the funeral, memorial, and burial
- Managing their personal affairs
- Cleaning out their home
- Handling all the details to honor and properly lay them to rest

In Task Mode, you don't have time to grieve. You're numb, just trying to get through each moment. You have family and friends around you, constant phone calls to make, and endless to-do lists. You're inundated, moving from one detail to another with only small pockets of time to focus on yourself.

But then the family leaves. The services are over. The phone calls stop, and you're forced to go back to your life after it just crashed. That's when it feels like the four walls are closing in. You feel alone, despondent, in despair, and sometimes, grief comes crashing in like a tidal wave.

During this process, throughout your grieving process, **Grief Brain** is a constant companion. Your mind feels cloudy, like walking around in a foggy room. You're forgetful, unfocused, and your nervous system is in a state of overwhelm because of the emotional and physiological stress of trying to process your loss.

This too is normal. All of it makes grief feel like it's consuming you. In those moments, cry out to Jesus. There's power in your voice crying out, and I don't just mean physically crying (which is healthy too), I mean literally shouting His name: "Jesus!"

When this happens, your nervous system is over-stimulated and doesn't know what to do with the pain. Crying out shifts the heavens and ushers in your breakthrough. But also, doing the work will too. The Bible talks about faith without works being dead. Sometimes in the church, we pray a lot, as we should. But sometimes what's missing is the action behind those prayers.

We have to work our faith. Grief is no different. If we are drowning, we can't just pray we won't drown. We have to physically help ourselves and cry out for others who have the power to assist us. During these times, it's so important to have an outlet, a way to release the pain instead of letting it swallow you whole.

We need Jesus and **Resiliency Tools.**

Resiliency Tools are like a toolkit. They are practical things you can use to get through hard times and bounce back. They help you handle the stress, weight, pain, or setbacks of grief (and life). We literally need Jesus to do the healing. We also have to surround ourselves with a tribe, a circle of support to help us navigate this type of pain, especially when the walls are closing in.

Don't have a circle of support? You're in for a treat. You can find one! It's healthy and perfectly acceptable to have spiritual support, but also human support to help us. God works in teams, and we don't heal in isolation. God created it so we heal in connection with others.

I'm not saying that alone time to allow God to process your pain isn't necessary, because it is. But there's a fine balance. Too much isolation gives the enemy access and can turn into his playground. Remember, one can put a thousand to flight, but two can put ten thousand to flight.

God created us to heal in connection. When the walls are closing in, we have to find support not only from The Lord, but in community to help us process the pain. I spent decades in complete ignorance, like most of us, unaware of the resources out here to help you process grief.

I had no idea how much silently suffering in grief was impacting my body. I've been between 130–145 lbs most of my life, but in my early 20s, my weight began to shift when I was graduating college. At my heaviest, after giving birth to my youngest daughter, I reached 325 lbs.

It wasn't until I started to tackle my weight and blog about my morbid obesity journey that I unearthed, through writing, a lifetime of grief. Like we said before: your body remembers. Your mind remembers too. It was a combination of a silent emotional unraveling, unexplained weight gain, and emerging illness that forced me to dig deep and care for myself before grief killed me.

How many times do we put on a façade that we're okay, conquering the world, while silently collapsing? It wasn't until I started to confront some of the pain I was feeling that I unearthed a lifetime of grief.

Here are some statistics on how grief impacts the body:

- People who are grieving experience 20–30% more sleep disturbances such as insomnia compared to those not grieving (Medical News Today, Mary West, Dec. 20, 2022).
- Around 40% of grieving individuals report physical symptoms like headaches, chest pain, stomach aches, or muscle tension (UCLA Health, Maanasi Kademani, Feb. 21, 2024).
- Grief can weaken the immune system for up to six months, making people more vulnerable to colds, flu, and infections (UCLA Health, Maanasi Kademani, Feb. 21, 2024; Immunize Nevada, 2023).

I had no idea about the concept of **Grief Work**. Grief Work is being intentional about processing your grief, not just allowing it to sit inside you. It means actively doing something with the pain in a healthy way so you can recover and move through it, instead of getting stuck in it.

I also had no idea about **Grief Movement**. Grief Movement is the ability to process grief that's stuck in your body through movement, breath, and sound.

Then I learned there was such a thing as a **Grief Coach. A Certified Grief Coach** is a companion who walks alongside you on this grief journey. They educate, listen, support, and helping you gain tools to navigate grief so you're not doing it alone.

After the pandemic, many online grief support groups emerged. One program I always recommend is Tender Hearts at Grief.com, a compassionate community of courageous grievers that I also help moderate under its founder, David Kessler.

Other in-person **grief support groups** include Compassionate Friends, GriefShare, The Dougy Center, Grief Recovery Institute, and many more. You can type "grief support near me" into your favorite search engine and find lists, or even ask AI to help with your search.

The self-care piece is really important during these moments when the walls feel like they're closing in. Ask yourself:

- Do you have a circle of support right now?
- Do you have someone safe to talk to?
- Can you do something physical to help get the energy and pain out of your body?

Some practical examples:
- Visiting rage rooms where you can safely smash things and release anger
- Going to an open field to yell and bellow out emotions
- Attending church services where you can cry out to God, scream, and let it all out
- Doing kickboxing or boxing, taking it out on a punching bag

These physical actions can help your body process pain instead of letting it stay trapped inside. The truth is, the walls will feel like they're closing in at times. That's normal.

But you can prepare for these moments. You can't prepare for everything, but like my mother always taught me: forewarned is forearmed. Since grief will be your forever companion, you have to learn about it so you can grow with it instead of it consuming you.

Jesus + **Resiliency Tools** + Self-Care go hand in hand.

You can have all Jesus but not practice practical tools, and find yourself stuck in a rut. You can have all practical tools but no Jesus, and you'll still be missing the spiritual peace and wholeness only He can give.

Faith without works is dead. Applying the Word of God, prayer, and practical tools together is essential in surviving the storms of grief, especially when the walls feel like they're caving in.

But even at our best efforts, with all the practical tools, the number one thing that binds everything together is Jesus. There is solace in Christ. Call out His name, and He will answer you.

I know you may not feel like praying. That's okay. Find pockets of time, tiny moments, to lean into your faith, because it's the only thing that will truly help you survive the storm. This is a season to strengthen your faith, or discover what you truly believe. Grief will either break your faith or make it resilient, but either way, it takes work.

If all you can do is:

- Reach for Him in small pockets of time
- Listen to the Word of God as you sit still

- Play worship music
- Have someone pray with you (or even call a trusted Christian prayer line)

Then do that, and also learn to pray for yourself. YouTube is a great resource for:

- Christian meditations
- Soothing worship music
- Guided prayers

These can help calm your nervous system, which often goes into overdrive trying to protect you.

Know this: When it feels like the four walls are closing in, that's normal. But Jesus is standing with you. He's pushing the walls back. He won't let them consume you.

I want you to know, I'm proud of you today, even if you're not proud of yourself. Show yourself compassion. Breathe. Just keep breathing, one second at a time. That's courage.

I love you and I'm thinking about you.

With love,
Ke'Shawn

SCRIPTURE

"And The Lord breathed life into them..." **(Ezekiel 37:9 –10, NIV).**

"When the enemy comes in like a flood, the Spirit of The Lord will lift up a standard against him" **(Isaiah 59:19, NIV).**

REFLECTION

Right now, only God can do what you need. We can do all the practical things (and we should), but to get through this season, you need to be spiritually anchored. Strengthen your spirit man. When your spirit is strong, your body and soul can follow but also, remember, faith without works is dead. Your self-care and finding support is your first act of worship in overcoming when the enemy comes in like a flood.

Jesus is standing with you, just like Daniel in the lions' den. He will hold back the lions. He will hold up the walls. He will never let them crash in on you. Have faith. Keep believing. Cry out in your distress. He will answer and deliver you.

REFLECTION QUESTIONS

- In what ways do you feel like the four walls are caving in?
- What can you do to keep from being swallowed by the moment?
- What can help anchor you through this season?
- Who is in your circle of support?

- What ways can you process grief that feels stuck in your body?
- Where can you research and commit to finding a tribe or circle of support if there is no one locally?

PRAYER

Father God, in the name of Jesus, I thank You for this day. I thank You that though the mountains may shake and the hills may be removed, Your unfailing love for me will never be shaken, and Your covenant of peace will never be removed.

Lord, You have compassion on me. No weapon formed against me shall prosper. I speak to the wind and the waves in my soul: Peace, be still. I thank You, Jesus, that You speak to my nervous system right now. I speak shalom over my job, my finances, my family, my mind, my body, my spirit and every circumstance concerning me.

I declare divine order over my life. Waves, be quiet. Wind, be still. Peace, I receive You now. Father, You will also help me find practical tools to help me in times of distress. You will lead me to a tribe that can support me: a community in my time of need. Thank You for going ahead of me and aligning what's needed in my life.

I shall live and not die, and see the salvation, healing, wholeness, and deliverance of The Lord while I'm in the land of the living. Help me to help myself and find the tools that can process my pain and lean into healing. I love You, and thank You for guiding my steps and quieting my storm.

In Jesus' mighty name, Amen.

DAY 21
JOURNAL

_____

_____

_____

_____

_____

_____

_____

_____

_____

_____

_____

_____

_____

_____

_____

_____

_____

_____

_____

_____

_____

_____

_____

— DAY 22 —

Show Yourself Compassion

*T*hat **inner critic** can be the worst.

You ever have that voice in your head that's tearing you down, calling you an idiot, stupid, blaming you for things? Yeah, that's the Inner Critic. The inner critic is that harsh voice inside your head that makes you feel guilty, ashamed, or condemned. It tells you you're not good enough, you failed, or you should have done more.

For us believers, that's straight up the devil. Remember, he is the accuser of the brethren, going before the Father day after day, hurling accusations. But what happens when you embrace those thoughts? You begin to believe those lies. You embrace the guilt, the shame, and the condemnation.

HOW DOES THIS SHOW UP IN YOUR GRIEF?

It shows up by feeling responsible for our loved one's death. It shows up on days when we judge our grief, when we tell ourselves we should be further along. It shows up when unexpected emotions appear. Grief bursts are those moments when your grief shows up without your permission and you shut it down only to tell yourself, "Toughen up, buttercup! Ain't nobody got time for tears, feelings, emotions. Get it together!"

What about when we cry and judge ourselves harshly, convincing ourselves it's a sign of weakness? What about sadness, have you ever been mad at yourself for being sad? What about the brave face you feel you have to put on for others, for the sake of not feeling vulnerable, or avoiding the sad stares, so you just pretend you're good? What about judging yourself on the would'ves, could'ves, should'ves, or regrets?

Here's the hard truth: a lot of times in grief, we're not good. Tears are our way of healing, not a sign of weakness. Not being okay is, in fact, okay, especially after losing someone we love. Although those things are normal, we can lack compassion for ourselves. We are our harshest critics, and sometimes how we talk to ourselves is terrible.

For me, my journey of grief hasn't always been about death. It's been about **Loss**, a change I didn't want, an adjustment I didn't want to make, or a **New Normal** I didn't choose. A new normal is the life you have to live after everything familiar has changed. It's learning to keep going when what once was, no longer is.

SELF-BLAME AND HEALTH

What about the times you've been sick, and sometimes your sickness came as a result of overeating or eating something you shouldn't have? What about the times you abuse yourself mentally, physically and emotional for making mistakes or having regrets?

For me, I had a tremendous amount of self-blame as it relates to my health, specifically morbid obesity and the health issues that arose from it. As I've said before, most of my life I was a size 13, 140 lbs. But in my early 20s, before graduating college, I began to put on weight unexpectedly, not knowing what was going on. It wasn't anything I was eating or drinking.

Only later, through therapy, journaling, blogging my journey, and overcoming obesity, did I learn that I was suffering from a lifetime of grief, **unexpressed grief** that was silently killing me and manifesting in my body.

During my journey of overcoming obesity, I truly beat myself up for anything I thought contributed to it, anything I'd done to cause it, I beat myself up mercilessly. When I became pregnant with my daughter, before that time, I was trying to overcome obesity. I always vigorously tried to take off the weight.

I exercised every day, I watched what I ate; I was not reckless in regards to my body. But with my best efforts, I could not take it off and keep it off.

So when I became pregnant unexpectedly, I was aggressively working to lose weight. It was my goal to prepare to have a baby and lose the weight first so it could be safe. But God said otherwise. SURPRISE. It was time for her to come.

Everything in me, the inner critic, the accuser of the brethren, the devil himself, convinced me I was a terrible person. "It's all your fault," he said. "God is mad at you. You didn't lose the weight He told you to lose, shame on you. He told you what He was expecting, and you were not prepared."

PREGNANCY AND TORMENT

I spent my entire pregnancy grief-stricken, feeling like God was mad at me. I was unprepared, and I was not in His will because I had allowed myself to get that big and wasn't ready when He called me to give birth.

So my heart complications, my lymphdema, and perhaps the close calls to losing her, all of it, I thought was my fault. During my traumatic delivery, I overheard the doctors in the teaching school at my door telling the students, "This patient is a candidate for a heart attack, hypertension, diabetes, everything, because she's morbidly obese."

Any chance the enemy got to reinforce, "You're a loser. It's your fault. If you lose your baby, it's your fault," he was working overtime, and because I had embraced the lies and truly felt guilty and at fault, the enemy had an open house to torment me. That was the epitome of grief.

HAVE YOU EVER?...

Have you ever had the enemy try to convince you or blame you for things that were outside your control? Have you ever made a mistake and the enemy keeps drilling in that it's all your fault? Do you ever talk to yourself so terribly that you tell yourself you should have done better?

I'm here to tell you: the world calls it the inner critic, but what I know to be true is that it's straight up the devil's work, and a lot of times, we buy into it. So I'm here to tell you today: if you were God, you would have prevented whatever happened, but you were not, and you couldn't.

GOD'S COMPASSION

Even with addiction, even with health complications, and with our best efforts, we all suffer from some form of trauma, hurt, pain, or inner wound that prevents us from doing better. We're struggling, and we don't have any mercy toward ourselves.

As I've said before, we don't know what we don't know. God is not like that. He's not looking at you, judging what you did or didn't do. He simply calls you and me to come.

He desires to forgive us where we have fallen short. He wants to show us compassion, to let us know that at our best, we're still fallen human beings. We have limited capacity, capabilities, knowledge, understanding, and sometimes will and strength.

There are just going to be some giants we can't slay. There are going to be some things in life we will be helpless to do or prevent. There are going to be some afflictions in our bodies caused by our eating or when we indulge in things that are not good for us. Sometimes we try to stop and we can't, and sometimes we have absolutely no control over them.

There will be afflictions that we didn't cause at all, but we'll blame ourselves. There will be giants we thought we should have conquered, secret sins that we wish we could change. At our best efforts, there will still be some strongholds in our lives that that only Jesus can break.

BE YOUR OWN FRIEND

So when you find yourself allowing the enemy to use you to shame you, I want you to be the friend to yourself that Jesus would be to you. Be the friend you would be to someone else. Encourage yourself that way. You would never tell an overweight friend, "You're so fat. Look what you did to yourself. You should know better."

Nor would you tell a loved one who has cancer, "Why are you in bed all the time? Why are you so sad? Get up and do something. Make yourself feel better instead of sitting around wallowing and being sick all the time."

Isn't that how we talk to ourselves? Or, "Look at you. You should have never done that. Stupid. You should have known better."

You would never say to a friend, "You caused your loved one to die because you didn't do what you were supposed to do."

God doesn't talk to us like that either. Be the Godly friend you would be to someone else. As my mommy says, be kind to yourself. When the enemy comes at you with lies, counter them with the truth of God's Word. Be your own advocate. Come to your own defense like you would for a friend.

You would never allow someone from the outside to speak to your friend like that, so stand up for yourself and shut the devil down.

ENCOURAGEMENT

I've spent my life guilty over what I couldn't control in my body and the things that came as a result. So I encourage you, I want you to know I'm proud of you. I want you to know it's okay that you're not perfect. You go ahead and cry.

No matter where you find yourself, in your health, your body, or your appearance, I'm proud of you. I want you to know how amazing you are. I want you to know you did show up for your family, your friends, and in this life. I want you to know you did your best, even if your best was just an inkling or didn't feel good enough. It was what you knew to be your best, and if there's room for better, even if your loved one has passed, you get to pay it forward.

God is a great reconciler of broken things. Although we can't change the past, we can take the pain of the past to make something in the future better. You are perfect just as you are. Even if you don't think you're doing grief well, I want to encourage you, I think you're doing great.

You showed up today, in your own way, whatever that looks like. I'm proud of all the efforts you're making, the strides you're taking. The fact that you're even reading this book now speaks volumes about how much you care about yourself and your healing.

More importantly than what I think, The Lord loves you. He's proud of you. He says,

"Come and pour out your guilt, shame, condemnation, all those things the enemy is accusing you of. I want you to know I'm not mad at you. I'll say it again, I'm not mad at you. I love and accept you just as you are.

Come and allow Me to console you. I want to comfort your regrets and pains, your burdens. I see you, and you are perfect, beautiful, and My baby. I love you with My everything, and I'll always forgive you.

Forgive yourself. My Son died so forgiveness is available. So today, I breathe My breath of love and comfort over you."

WHO YOU ARE IN HIM

He wants to remind you who you are in Him: You are the apple of His eye. A jewel in His crown. A child who is forgiven. A child redeemed by The Lord. Despite how you feel, you are victorious.

I love you, and I'm asking you to show yourself compassion as you would show compassion to a friend. Don't beat yourself up, not one day longer. This practice may take time, but over time, it will begin healing you, little by little, and healing your land. Be kind to yourself.

I'm so proud of you, even if you are not proud of yourself.

I love you and I'm thinking about you.

With love,
Ke'Shawn

SCRIPTURE

"Then I heard a loud voice in heaven say: 'Now have come the salvation and the power and the kingdom of our God, and the authority of his Messiah. For the accuser of our brothers and sisters, who accuses them before our God day and night, has been hurled down'" **(Revelation 12:10, NIV).**

"The Lord is compassionate and gracious, slow to anger, abounding in love" **(Psalm 103:8, NIV).**

"Come, all you who are thirsty, come to the waters; and you who have no money, come, buy and eat! Come, buy wine and milk without money and without cost. Why spend money on what is not bread, and your labor on what does not satisfy? Listen, listen to me, and eat what is good, and you will delight in the richest of fare. Give ear and come to me; listen, that you may live. I will make an everlasting covenant with you, my faithful love promised to David" **(Isaiah 55:1-3, NIV).**

"For you created my inmost being; you knit me together in my mother's womb. I praise you because I am fearfully and wonderfully made; your works are wonderful, I know that full well. You know when I sit and when I rise; you perceive my thoughts from afar" **(Psalm 139:2, 13–14, NIV).**

"To the praise of his glorious grace, which he has freely given us in the One he loves" (Ephesians 1:6, NIV).
"God made him who had no sin to be sin for us, so that

in him we might become the righteousness of God" **(2 Corinthians 5:21, NIV).**

"'Come now, let us settle the matter,' says The Lord. 'Though your sins are like scarlet, they shall be as white as snow; though they are red as crimson, they shall be like wool'" **(Isaiah 1:18, NIV).**

REFLECTION

God invites us to come freely and receive all we need; without cost, without being perfect, or giving anything. He knows us intimately, from the very moment of our formation in the womb. Despite our mistakes, shortcomings, and failures, He accepts us fully, washes away our sins, and clothes us in righteousness through Jesus Christ.

The enemy may accuse and condemn, but God's love is abounding and His forgiveness is complete. We are called to come to Him, to be healed, and to show ourselves the same compassion He freely offers us.

Tear down your own walls with Him. You are safe. You don't need to hide; He accepts you as you are. Even if you find yourself falling, failing, or sinning, He wants to help you, not condemn you. The devil does that.

He's quick to listen, slow to anger, and He's not waiting to take vengeance on you because you sin. He wants to show you compassion, so come into His presence and let Him.

He wants to remind you that He is Father first, and what true parent wants to destroy his or her kid if they make a mistake–even when they infuriate us? Even when we discipline our children, don't we feel bad? Absolutely, and The Lord does too.

Abba Father desires you come to Him as you are; real, authentic, not hiding, so He can help and give you rest. Just come!

REFLECTION QUESTIONS

- What is the enemy whispering in your ear?
- What lies are you believing?
- What guilt, shame, or condemnation are you carrying?
- In what ways can you learn to let it go?
- How can you show yourself compassion today?

PRAYER

Father God, in the name of Jesus, I thank You for this day. I thank You that You don't treat me how I treat myself. I ask You for forgiveness for abusing me, for not talking to myself kindly, for not showing myself compassion, for guilting, shaming, blaming, and condemning myself.

Forgive me for coming into agreement with the devil and believing his lies and not refuting any of them. Wash over me with Your truth. Silence the voice of the enemy. I pray in the name of Jesus.

Holy Spirit, when the lies come in like a flood, speak truth over me. Speak truth in my sleep, in my dreams, in my coming in, and in my going out. I'm being tormented by guilt, shame, and condemnation of what I should have been doing and what I didn't do. I'm feeling shame and guilt over my behaviors and my actions that don't serve me well. I'm guilting, shaming, condemning, and beating myself up.

I am just sad that I am in a place in my life where I'm unable to help myself. So I cry out to You, Jesus. Help me!

In Jesus' name, throw me a lifeline. Supernaturally allow heaven to come to earth on my behalf and deliver me from the grips of Satan and the voices of the enemy, and I ask that You send all of heaven to surround me, to reinforce Your truth. Create in me a clean heart, renew within me a right spirit out of this sin and wickedness.

I thank You for my deliverance and victory.

In Jesus' mighty name, Amen.

DAY 22
JOURNAL

_____
_____
_____
_____
_____
_____
_____
_____
_____
_____
_____
_____
_____
_____
_____
_____
_____
_____
_____
_____
_____
_____
_____
_____
_____

Grief Changes You, and That's Okay!

Grief has a way of feeling like it ripped your soul into a thousand pieces, and it changes you. Do you feel like your loss has changed you? I'm almost certain you'd say, 100%. Here's a fact: You're no longer the same after losing someone you love and experiencing deep grief. The world, and sometimes even the people closest to you, don't understand that.

I remember when my dad, Pete, who raised me, died. Everything in me felt like ten tractor trailers had run me over. I was in a constant daze. My heart was enraged. I was a ticking time bomb.

It was just my mom and me now. After my grandmother died, one by one, some of my immediate family moved, and my sister eventually went away to college. It was just me and my mom on a daily basis for many years, and my sister came back home on vacations.

My mother, as a divorced parent, did everything she could to stabilize me along with my sister. She wanted to create a sense of normalcy in my adolescence, but they both couldn't shield me or control death, grief, and all the secondary losses we went through as a family.

But God! Over time, He started rebuilding our immediate family again. My sister came home from college, we were older, and now God was giving us something new. It was my mom, my big sister, my dad, Pete, and myself. Although Pete helped raise me, I was blessed to have two dads: my biological dad, along with extended family, and a host of best friends and their families who became my adopted family.

It was not the original crew, but The Lord was doing a new thing. I began to feel that same family fullness and the feeling I had as a little kid with my grandparents, uncles, mother, and sister, the original crew. My sister and I were young adults. We were all serving The Lord, enjoying fish Fridays, family outings, parties, making memories, and celebrating holidays.

Pete was our forever teenager. He was off his rocker sometimes, but he was a strong tower, a constant support for all of us, and ended up being my best friend. He was someone we could always count on. With him being the man of the house, we felt covered and safe. I was also grateful for my biological dad, who remained a steady part of my life. He was another source of strength and love that reminded me God had truly surrounded me with layers of family.

My life was full, and every day I relished coming home. It took years to bring that full circle, that sense of community, and it brought my heart so much joy that we were all together and able to see what God could do.

Then, out of nowhere, my dad, Pete died. I finally had the same essence of family as a kid, now as a young adult, and BAM, for him to die. OMG! My world came crashing down, AGAIN! Everything felt foreign and strange, like it did when I was a kid.

But no matter what just happened, I did, we did,

what we knew to do. My mom went back to work, and so did I, and no matter how I was feeling, life went on; shattered soul and all.

I need to pause and share how horrible that feels, when your world is crushed and you just have to move on and try to go back to normal!!!! WHHHAAATT!!! ARRRGHHH! OMG!!!!! RAGING!!!

I was forced to take care of my responsibilities. There was no opting out or checking out. I had to make sure my mother and I were okay, not allowing my grief to consume me to the point where I couldn't carry my weight. It wasn't Mom and Dad holding me up anymore like in college or being a kid. I had to hold myself, and I had to support my mother, too.

Don't get me wrong. My mother has always been a soldier, a straight-up rock of Gibraltar, my biggest support. Even after losing her husband, she still was a support. But now, her protector was no longer watching over her. I had to take on watching and protecting her too, and the worry I carried wanting her to be OK.

My sister had just moved out of state shortly before Pete passed, and came home often. But on the day-to-day, the weight and pressure to stand strong, to reciprocate all my mother poured into me, fell on my shoulders. Even with all her strength, we had to be strong for each other.

Everything in me changed. I remember someone saying to me: "I'm a little worried about you. You're different," while we were hanging out enjoying ourselves. "You no longer have that light and spark inside you. It's like you're just going through the motions, like the real you, that glimmer, it's not there anymore."

I didn't think I was different. I was just laughing and joking like I normally did. Of course, my emotions and everything in me were crushed, but I thought I was doing a good job showing up the same. I was a little taken back by the comment. It was definitely meant in love and out of concern. But for me, I wasn't sure how I felt about that concern, or what to do with it, or how to fix it.

I began questioning, "Am I different?"

I sat with that for some time, wrestling with it. Everything around me changed, but I thought I did a good job trying to stay the same. I couldn't put my finger on what I was feeling or what I was thinking. It left me questioning, have I changed? I kind of felt bad that someone thought my spark had left.

What do I need to do to FIX MYSELF and get back to normal?

Here's what I've learned in my grief trainings: Grief changes you, and THAT'S OK! You're not supposed to be the same after losing someone you truly loved. You will not be the same after a traumatic loss, and THAT'S OK.

Depending on how your loved one died, and how close you were, you're not supposed to be "okay." Your world has turned upside down. Not only do you have to deal with the reality that your loved one is no longer physically here, you also have to deal with all the losses:
- shattered hopes and dreams
- lost visions for the future
- and all the secondary losses that come when they're gone.

That's far too much for a human heart to process. So

yes, you will absolutely change after grief, and it will take time to find your footing again. There is no going back to "normal." From the moment that everything changed after death, every day moving forward, you think only about how to live, how to survive each moment. I had to get acclimated to a New Normal, a life lived every day without my dad.

How to adjust to all those missed moments and secondary losses, and if you have kids or loved ones depending on you, it feels even heavier. You're not just thinking about yourself, you're trying to be strong for them, even when you can't be strong for yourself.

I had to make peace with the fact that I'm different now. Everything about me shifted. Life became about surviving, taking one small step in front of the other.

Another thing I learned is this: Our grief can make people uncomfortable.

They don't know how to engage with this "new" version of us. They want us to smile, to get out of the house, to "do something." While that's well-intentioned, sometimes we don't even know who we are anymore. Sometimes we don't want to laugh. Sometimes nothing feels funny. Everyone grieves differently, and when people truly love you, they desperately want to fix what you're feeling.

But the truth is, no one can fix this. Only God can. So forgive me if I'm not smiling, I don't feel like going out, my mood is sober and sad, or I look like I have no spark left in me.

Forgive me if, truth be told, sometimes it feels like I've died, too. Grief can feel that deep, like it's killing you on the inside. But if we remember the truth: The core of grief is love.

You loved, and you lost, and that love still aches so deeply it feels unbearable. Grief is only present because love was real, and loss has broken your heart. So I encourage you today: if you feel like you're dying on the inside after losing someone you deeply loved, hold onto Jesus. He is the lifeline that will carry you when you feel like you can't carry yourself. Let His presence breathe life into the places that feel empty and broken.

Sometimes, it does feel like it's killing you and eating you alive. If you no longer feel the same, perhaps you're not. You're not supposed to be the same. I validate what you're feeling. I hold space for you even when the world doesn't. It's okay if others are uncomfortable with your grief.

At the end of the day, the only One who truly needs to "get" your grief is God. A lot of this journey can only be walked with Him, by yourself. So when friends and family tell you:

"You're different, you're not the same, you don't laugh or cry like you used to, everything about you has changed,"

Tell them, "I'm sorry my loss makes you sad. I'm sorry you feel helpless because you want to fix it for me. I'm sorry if I can't be to you what I used to be. I'm sorry that my loss has broken your heart too. I acknowledge your grief as well."

For others who may be judging how I'm grieving, "I'm sorry if my grief makes you uncomfortable. I'm sorry I'm not the same, but I shouldn't be. Please just pray me through as I heal and recover, one day at a time."

Another truth is that sometimes, in this type of grief, relationships will change too. Sometimes, relationships can't survive the change. Some people won't be able to meet you where you are, and there will be a sense of disconnect between you both. This too is normal.

Allow time, God, and healing to take its course. Sometimes with relationships, it's a reason, season, or lifetime. Some people will not always walk with you all the way, or vice versa. That too is OK.

The one thing we can rest in with our entire life shifting is GOD in Christ Jesus. He will always walk with you no matter the change or season, and He never changes no matter where we find ourselves.

God is walking this road with you. I don't know when, I don't know how, but one millisecond at a time, He will breathe new life into you. He will restore you as you put your hope and trust in Him.

You will find your footing again. It may not go back to how things were, but God will settle and stabilize you again. It may take time, a lot of time, so be patient with yourself and know, you are doing your best and God is proud.

I love you and I'm thinking about you.

With love,
Ke'Shawn

SCRIPTURE

"Then he said to me, 'Prophesy to these bones and say to them, Dry bones, hear the word of The Lord! ... I will make breath enter you, and you will come to life'" **(Ezekiel 37:4–5, NIV)**.

"Therefore, if anyone is in Christ, the new creation has come: The old has gone, the new is here!" **(2 Corinthians 5:17, NIV)**.

"...to bestow on them a crown of beauty instead of ashes, the oil of joy instead of mourning, and a garment of praise instead of a spirit of despair" **(Isaiah 61:3, NIV)**.

"Comfort, comfort my people, says your God." **(Isaiah 40:1, NIV)**.

"And I will ask the Father, and he will give you another advocate to help you and be with you forever—the Spirit of truth" **(John 14:16–17, NIV)**.

"Though my father and mother forsake me, The Lord will receive me" **(Psalm 27:10 NIV)**.
"There is a time for everything, and a season for every activity under the heavens" **(Ecclesiastes 3:1, NIV)**.

REFLECTION

Things in your life may feel strange and different, and they should. People don't show up the same. It feels quiet and abnormal. Dark and cloudy.

Right now, everyone can't understand or go on this journey with you. Only God can heal your broken places. You may feel shattered, broken into a thousand pieces, beyond repair. Your faith may feel diminished, or maybe it's been strengthened.

If your faith is shaken, I pray The Lord will send signs to breathe life into you again, like He did with those dry bones, to remind you He is near even in your pain. He knows your loss because He, too, endured loss, the tragic loss of His Son.

But just as He restored His Son, He gave Him beauty for His ashes. He promises to restore you. He will send the Holy Spirit to cover you and send helpers on earth to assist you. The last season of your life has changed, that's heartbreaking.

One millisecond at a time, He will bring light back to your days and joy to your heart again. It'll take time. Crying may endure for the night, but He promises joy, one day at a time, will come in the morning.

Continue to pray for strength to hold on. I'll be praying for you, too, and know when you let go, His grip tightens, and He will not let you go.

REFLECTION QUESTIONS

- How have you changed since the passing of your loved one?
- In what ways have people expressed concern about how you've changed?
- How can you honor your change and advocate for yourself when others think you should grieve differently?

PRAYER

Father God, in the name of Jesus, I thank You for this day, even though it feels cloudy, even though it feels lonely. Your Word says You will be with me. You will not leave me as an orphan. You will receive me.

I have changed. I feel empty, hollow, lost, dark, angry, and full of rage. Holy Spirit, fall fresh on me. Grant me peace. Give me strength to block out the voices of the world and the lies of the enemy that bring guilt, condemnation, and shame for where I am.

Send the right people to speak life over me. Speak to my family and friends who are concerned and show them how to support me.

I feel alone, but You promised that if I draw near to You, You will draw near to me. So I'm drawing near. Lord, carry me because I cannot carry myself.

Every moment is a struggle. I lean on Your everlasting arms to hold me, to sustain me, to carry me through.

Thank You for doing it.

In Jesus' mighty name, Amen.

DAY 23
JOURNAL

You Shall Live and Not Die

When your loved one died, did it feel like you died too? Most of us can say yes, because grief and loss can feel like it destroys everything inside. I remember going back to work and, as I've shared before, that feeling of rage kept coming up. I didn't know what to do with myself. I felt like getting in my car and just driving with no destination in sight.

But I had responsibilities. I had my mom. I had God's hand on my life and an assignment He wanted me to fulfill in spite of what I was going through. My grief felt like cancer eating me alive. It felt like it was destroying me from the inside out.

All I could feel was anger and rage. I didn't know what to do with those feelings. As much as I loved God and prayer, I didn't want to pray. I didn't want to sit at The Lord's feet like I customarily did. Every day, I used to spend time with The Lord, let Him speak to me, journal, and pour out my heart. But after my loss, I was scared to death to do that, because I knew if I sat with Him, I would be forced to feel.

I wasn't ready to feel. For some people, it's staying busy with work or tasks. For me, it was staying busy and avoiding prayer time with The Lord. I remember attending a prayer conference my spiritual mother hosted every year. They invited people to come forward for prayer.

I went up. I'll never forget the woman who prayed for me. God spoke through her: "You can't die too. You can't die too. There's work for you to do. You're assigned and anointed for great work. You can't die. I don't know what happened to you, but whatever it is, you can't allow yourself to die too."

I went back to my table while prayer was still going on. The Spirit of God was hovering over that place. I closed my eyes, and supernaturally, I saw enormous nostrils hovering over me, larger than life. I saw smoke, breath, coming out of them, breathing on me. It was the Lord's breath, breathing life back into me.

Every death I've endured in my lifetime has found a way to kill a piece of me inside. The closer I was to the person, and depending on how they died, the deeper it felt like a part of me was dying too. When my dad, Pete died, everything in me felt like it was dying. When I sat by my uncle's ICU bed in his last moments, he was like a brother to me, everything in me felt like it was dying.

My grandmother, "Mommy," my grandfather, "Daddy," when they died, they each took a piece of me with them. Then, all the other family members I adored. Yeah, they too, took a piece of me. That particular day at the prayer conference, when The Lord breathed over me, I didn't realize I was dying on the inside. Because life didn't stop, I didn't have time to think of what my insides were doing.

I ran an office, I was successful, I traveled the world and tried to the best of my ability to enjoy life. I didn't realize that for every death, a part of me was being chipped away. I didn't know I was a dead girl walking, but I showed the world I was doing just fine. I had no idea I was coding and needed resuscitation. It wasn't until that encounter with Him that I finally realized what was happening to me, and in that moment, everything shifted.

I realized in that moment: I had to allow God to breathe life back into me.

Because of my avoidance of prayer, my reluctance to dig my feet into my faith, it was killing me. I want to encourage you today: I know you may feel like after such a loss you're dying too. You know what: your loss may be killing you too, like it was killing me, choking you alive. I know you feel like you don't know how you'll ever recover from the devastation you're feeling.

As a matter of fact, you know you won't ever recover from this place. I know you don't know what to do with yourself, where to go from here, or even how to think about your future. It just won't ever be the same. I know, and for that, I'm so sorry. In this moment, I'm truly sorry you find yourself here and this is a part of your story.

Right now, you're just trying to survive the moment. But wherever you are right now, wherever you find yourself, The Lord wants to share this with you too: **You. Can't. Die. Too!**

For some of us, we have kids. For others, we have parents, we have responsibilities, and if we stop moving completely, we'll sink under.

But most importantly, beyond all those things, God wants to remind you: You can't die too. I know your life doesn't have the same meaning without your loved one, but your life still has purpose and meaning too. You have a unique fingerprint on this earth.

It's understandable if you feel like you have no purpose, hope, or faith without your loved one. It's okay to feel that way, and you should. You can't help where you are right now. But this is what The Lord wants you to hear: As scary as it feels, as hard as it feels, go into the presence of God and let Him breathe life back into you.

You may not feel like you want to live, but God still has plans for you even in the midst of your world collapsing. Don't allow the enemy to steal, kill, or destroy the legacy your loved one left, the legacy that still gets to live through you, in their honor. In grief and loss, we face a choice. We either allow grief to swallow us whole, or one millisecond at a time, one choice at a time, we begin to take small steps that honor our loved ones even in our deep grief. As we do, God takes our pain and turns it into purpose.

This doesn't happen overnight. It takes time to merge the pain, search for meaning, and figure out, "What do I do now?"

But hear me, God is no respecter of persons. If He resurrected me from dying inside, He will do the same for you. I know our losses are not the same, and I have no idea what you've just been through, so I'm not saying it flippantly.

But I've seen and spoken to countless people, heard so many tumultuous stories of how grief, loss, and horrific pain broke them. In every situation, God turned their nightmare into meaning. The Lord wants you to know, He will breathe new life into you. He will give you new strength. He will not do it for others and not do it for you. Cry out to Him with everything in you, and He will rescue you.

Acceptance and meaning don't happen overnight. It's a journey and it may take a lot of time, courage, prayer, and support. But He specializes in miracles and desires to do a miracle in you. He didn't bring you this far to leave you now. He won't ever.

I love you and I'm thinking about you.

With love,
Ke'Shawn

SCRIPTURE

"Then The Lord God formed a man from the dust of the ground and breathed into his nostrils the breath of life, and the man became a living being" (**Genesis 2:7, NIV**).

"This is what the Sovereign Lord says to these bones: I will make breath enter you, and you will come to life" (**Ezekiel 37:5, NIV**).

REFLECTION

It's in these desperate moments that God shows His miraculous power. When the Egyptians chased the Israelites and they stood trapped between the water and their enemy, they trusted God, and He parted the sea and brought them through. Wherever you are right now, I know it's hard to believe, but even with the faith of a mustard seed, you can speak life over yourself: "I shall live and not die and see the salvation of The Lord."

Speak it again and again because faith comes from hearing, and hearing the Word of God. Declare His Word over your life. It will not return empty. It will accomplish what He has spoken and fulfill its purpose in you. I decree and declare, you shall live and not die and see the salvation and miracle of The Lord. I'm believing for a miracle for you right now in Jesus' name.

REFLECTION QUESTIONS

- In what ways have parts of you felt like they died when your loved one passed away?
- What small ways can you begin to speak life back into yourself today?

- What small steps can you take to honor their life even in the midst of your pain?

PRAYER

Father God, in the name of Jesus, I pray right now. Everything in me feels like it's dying, but Your Word says, "I shall live and not die and declare the salvation of The Lord." So I speak it over myself now; over and over again: I shall live and not die and declare the wondrous works of The Lord. I shall live and not die and see the miraculous hand of God in my life. I speak life.

The breath of The Lord is breathing on me right now, resurrecting everything dead within me. I shall live and not die. I will see Your promises fulfilled. I will witness Your salvation. My loved one will not die in vain. They will live on through me.

I will fulfill my assignment. I will finish my race for their honor and for Your glory, Lord Jesus. I declare it is so.

In Jesus' mighty name, Amen.

DAY 24
JOURNAL

_____

_____

_____

_____

_____

_____

_____

_____

_____

_____

_____

_____

_____

_____

_____

_____

_____

_____

_____

_____

_____

_____

_____

_____

Old Wounds Complicate Grief

Have you ever been in grief, and out of nowhere, a deep hurt or pain from your past crept in? You're like, "Where did this come from? I haven't thought about that in years!" What about losing someone, and out of nowhere, the pain of loss from another person that passed resurfaces?

For me, for every death, it felt like it would open up Pandora's box. What I didn't know was that this was normal. David Kessler's model of *6 Needs of the Grieving* mentions that this part of grief is normal and common. **Old wounds** will resurface, complicating your current process of grief.

Old Wounds in grief are unresolved hurts, past traumas, or earlier losses that resurface when a new loss occurs. These can include childhood rejection, past abuse, unfinished conflicts, or even the earlier death of a loved one. Old wounds often reawaken when grief reopens the heart, and they can complicate the current grieving process. Every time a loved one of mine died, I would get this pain on the side of my rib. It felt like a machete had sliced me, and it was always the same feeling whenever someone I was close to passed away.

When my Uncle David passed, God bless his soul, our family was heartbroken. He was a big part of my dad, Pete's life, the dad who raised me, and they were close. Whenever he was around, he always made his presence felt. Uncle David was sweet, kind, gentle, caring, calm, extremely smart, good with technology, and had a quiet humor.

As a child, whenever Uncle David visited, he'd make time to check on me, to see what I was up to. He took a genuine interest in my education and the things I was pursuing. We would often talk. He would often come sit in my room every time he came by and check on me.

After my dad, Pete, died, Uncle David and his family were still a big part of ours. So, when he abruptly passed, my heart was extremely broken. But what caught me off guard was that while grieving him, I found myself grieving my dad, Pete. It was like I lost my dad all over again.

My dad and his siblings were close-knit, and we all were connected and important to our family. Having Uncle David, not only did you feel the love from him and the family in his own right, but his presence brought me comfort. In some way, I still had a piece of my dad with us through his siblings and our extended family. But when Uncle David passed, it felt like losing twice, losing him and reliving the pain of losing my dad, Pete.

When my grandfather "Daddy" passed, that too felt like losing my grandmother all over again. They had both partnered to help my mom raise me. So even though we were grieving my grandfather, it brought up every feeling of losing my grandmother. It felt like losing them both again.

I could go on and on about my uncles, aunts, and extended family. That's the thing about grief, it's complex, and our relationships with one another are never isolated. With each person, our relationships are interconnected, filled with memories and legacy woven together in a rich tapestry of love. One person connects with the others and brings so many dynamics of grief.

Sometimes in grief, old wounds rise to the surface. Unfinished hurts, childhood memories, teenage pains, things you haven't thought about in years suddenly resurface. Losing one person can unlock memories and wounds you didn't even know were still there. David Kessler often says when someone asks where to begin healing, he responds: "Where are your **triggers**?"

Grief Triggers are sometimes called *Triggers in the Body.* They occur when something you see, smell, taste, touch, or witness brings your grief to the surface. These triggers, also known as heightened emotional responses, can manifest in the body and cause sadness, anxiety, fatigue, or even physical pain.

When old wounds surface in the midst of grief and loss, your grief is signaling something. It's letting you know there are other parts of you that need attention, other areas of your life that need healing. Although we may not like it, this can be a blessing in disguise, pointing us toward the deeper work needed to truly heal and close unfinished chapters.

You might be thinking: "I don't have time to deal with old wounds right now." I get it. I felt the same way. You're already trying to navigate your current grief, and now the past creeps in too. It feels overwhelming.

But what God has shown me is this: We can't pour from an empty cup. What we run from will pursue us. What we avoid will persist. It doesn't just hurt our souls, it can leave us emotionally stuck and even physically harm our bodies.

I encourage you today: Let the feelings flow. Don't run from it.

I know it's painful, but we must learn to grow curious when old pains spring up. Wherever you find old wounds that need healing, trust that God has provided resources to help. Seek out licensed professionals, therapists, grief coaches, and people equipped to walk with you through deep pain. If some wounds feel too painful to revisit, pray for courage. Pray for the boldness of a lion. Ask God to strengthen you to face whatever you must in order to find healing.

He's calling each of us to a place of healing and wholeness, and He will help you as you walk this out with Him. Also, be mindful that the enemy wants to keep you in cycles of suffering. It's important when we find these old wounds coming up again and again. It's God pointing out that this part of us needs attention, healing, or deliverance, to shut the door to Satan from taking advantage of that wound.

God's intention is always about life and healing. I encourage you, for the sake of your loss, your loved one's legacy, and your own purpose, face it with Jesus. Don't run one more single day. Don't allow these old wounds to consume you so much that you never find the transformative power it could possibly bring to your life and others.

I'm praying for your courage today. I too am going back down walkways that have been too painful. No one, and I mean no one, wants to walk those paths again. But sometimes, the only way out is through, and you can't heal what you don't feel. That wound won't leave unless you face it, but you don't have to do it alone.

Jesus died and took back the keys from Satan and hell so you can be free. Your freedom and transformation are on the other side of this pain. God's got you, and I'm so very proud of you.

I love you and I'm thinking about you.

With love,
Ke'Shawn

SCRIPTURE

"Be strong and courageous. Do not be afraid; do not be discouraged, for The Lord your God will be with you wherever you go" (**Joshua 1:9, NIV**).

"Fear not, for I am with you; be not dismayed, for I am your God; I will strengthen you, I will help you..." (**Isaiah 41:10, ESV**).

"Even though I walk through the darkest valley, I will fear no evil, for you are with me; your rod and your staff, they comfort me" (**Psalm 23:4, NIV**).

REFLECTION

In moments when old pain resurfaces, God reminds us to be strong and courageous. He is with us in both present grief and past wounds. As He told Joshua before facing great battles, He tells us today: Do not fear. I am with you. I will give you courage. I will make you whole again.

In Christ, it's possible to do it afraid. With heart pounding and knees quaking, you have what it takes to go down those darkened paths to your victory. Courage is not the absence of fear, it's in the doing that Christ strengthens you for the battle.

REFLECTION QUESTIONS

- What old wounds have resurfaced for you in the midst of your grief?
- What small steps can you take to begin speaking life and healing over those areas?
- How can you allow God and others to help you find wholeness?

PRAYER

Father God, in the name of Jesus, I'm trying to navigate my grief, and pain from my past keeps creeping in. I pray for courage to face whatever giants I need to face in order to experience the healing You have for me. I confess that I'm not bold enough.

I'm not courageous enough. I'm scared to face what I've already lived through once. But I know You are my strength. Strengthen me to confront what needs to be healed to dig my feet into faith and trust You to make me whole again.

I cut the soul ties of trauma of my past that haunt me and keep me hostage. In Jesus' name, the devil has been defeated and I overcome the enemy with the blood of the Lamb and the word of my testimony. You are with me and You will not leave me. Though I walk through the valley of the shadow of death, I will not be afraid, for You are with me, fighting for me and helping me overcome this battle. I thank You for hearing this prayer and answering it.

In Jesus' mighty name, Amen.

DAY 25
JOURNAL

_____

_____

_____

_____

_____

_____

_____

_____

_____

_____

_____

_____

_____

_____

_____

_____

_____

_____

_____

_____

_____

_____

_____

_____

_____

_____

Grief Manifesting in Your Body

*H*ave you ever been in deep grief and experienced migraines, sharp pains, aches, extreme weakness or fatigue, or even developed new health issues you couldn't explain? You're not imagining things. This part of grief is real. I had no idea there was such a strong connection between grief and how it impacts your physical body. That's normal, and I didn't understand it until I began my grief journey.

The one concept I was taught is that **The Body Keeps Score**. Grief and trauma live in the body, often showing up as inflammation, illness, aches, or other physical symptoms when unprocessed. The body remembers the effects of heartbreaks, pains, and traumas you have endured, even if you forget. The body never forgets.

As I previously mentioned, I remember during my senior year in college, I had always been a size 13. But suddenly, without changing my eating habits or lifestyle, I started gaining weight I couldn't explain. Fast-forward to before having my daughter, I had reached 325 pounds (from typically being 145 pounds), and that weight impacted everything: my pregnancy, delivery, my ability to live life fully, my self-esteem, self-worth, and self-love. Most importantly, it affected my mental health.

Again, grief moves beyond death. It's loss; loss of

self-esteem, mourning over who I used to be, how people treated me, unkind words, rejection. You name it, I've got stories for days of the loss and rejection I felt from obesity and losing my health.

Because of the extra weight, I developed lymphedema, plantar fasciitis, and even had heart complications during pregnancy that required medication. Not only did I endure illness, but also every time someone close to me passed away, I felt deep, sharp pain in my ribs, like I'd been sliced open. At the time, I didn't know, but that was grief living inside my body. It was how grief was manifesting.

It was manifesting in my ribs, and for every loss I stuffed in my soul, it manifested as weight in my body. It was like there was an entire war going on within, and my body was keeping score, responding through weight gain and inflammation. It wasn't until I became a **Certified Grief Educator** through David Kessler's program that I learned how powerfully grief can impact our health. I was introduced by David to Paul Denniston and a method called Grief Movement.

Grief Movement helps us notice where grief is stored in our bodies and gently release it through breathing, sound, and simple movements–often just from sitting in a chair.

This isn't therapy, it's not yoga, and it doesn't involve spirituality. It's simply a practical tool to help you physically identify and process where grief is manifesting and what it's doing to your body. While grief coaching and counseling deal with the emotions, grief movement deals with the body.

That understanding led me to become a **Grief Movement Guide**, someone who helps others gently release the heaviness that grief places on their bodies. If you understand stress, you know it can harm your body, and grief is the greatest stressor of all. It's no surprise that it can lead to unexplained illness and pain. You're not imagining it, the sickness, aches, and unexplained pains. Grief really does affect your body.

That's why, during this season, it's important to have a circle of support:

- Grief support groups
- Grief coaches
- Compassionate partners or friends
- And even **grief movement guides** like me, who can help you safely process what your body is carrying through gentle, practical steps.

God knows what we don't know and timed things in my life perfectly. At the tail end of my working with David Kessler, I transitioned to working with Paul Denniston, working on my certification for Grief Movement. Right as everything was transitioning, I was in excruciating pain. Out of nowhere, it was like I had influenza A times 1,000. I couldn't walk, bend any joints, or do anything.

My body was full of pain. I had little strength. I was despondent. But me being me, a warrior at heart, and me being a mom and wife, I had a family and had to keep going. I walked around wrecked in pain and no one knew a thing.

I had to keep being a mom. I still took my Grief Movement classes, still got my baby to school, to her activities. I still exercised and went to physical therapy. For me, whatever I was going through, I was not going to let it make me lay in bed helpless. I was bent on fighting back.

I did all of this extremely broken in spirit, soul, and body. My mental health was fragile. But in that moment of brokenness, God used the tools I was learning in Grief Movement to process my emotional pain and to help me notice where grief was stuck in my body so I could gently release it. I was angry at God, angry that this was happening to me.

Only to find out later, I was diagnosed with Lupus. I was really angry at God, angry at my loss of health to this magnitude. The same concepts, just like when I was pregnant with my daughter, I did everything I could to be in good health, and my health was failing me. Not only with obesity, now lupus.

Grief Movement was my saving grace. Through this process, I was able to confront the grief of my health loss, the extreme pain I was in, and the old grief that still needed healing. During class, I had quiet moments to cry out to God and use the tools I was given to release what I was feeling in real time. I was using my body to pray, **body prayers**, moving, breathing, and crying out in words. Even while I was sick, this practice brought me comfort and carried me through the devastation of my diagnosis.

My journey of education on grief was first for me to find my healing, then learning how to take my pain and turn it into purpose. I don't know your journey, if or how grief has affected your health. I don't know if you, like me, struggle in your body or feel any type of pain or limitation in your physical frame or your mind.

If you're in pain today, spirit, soul, or body, let's start with something simple: Let's take a moment to stop what we're doing and simply breathe.

What does deep breathing do? When you pause and intentionally breathe deeply, it signals to your brain that your body is safe. This helps calm your nervous system and begins releasing tension that grief can lock inside you. It activates the parasympathetic nervous system, helping your body shift out of fight-or-flight and return to a state of safety, peace and healing.

If you experience unexplained symptoms, know you are not alone. God can bring healing, not just to your broken heart but to your body as well. He can send you resources, tools, and people to walk with you so you don't carry this pain alone. There is help out there, don't be afraid to reach out.

Most people, myself included, feel like they can do this journey alone. But here's what's really happening: we're suffering in silence, slowly collapsing on the inside. God heals through connection with others and community. For all that you are going through, it's crucial that you find support. Find a place to talk and process, and, with Jesus, human support from a qualified person to walk with you through everything you are facing.

If therapy is not your thing, there is **Grief Peer-to-Peer Support, Grief Group Support, Grief Coaches,** and Christian counselors too. You're not alone in this. Not in the pain in your heart. Not in the pain in your body.

We're walking this road together, toward healing, wholeness, and life again, one moment at a time.

I love you, and I'm thinking about you.

With love,
Ke'Shawn

SCRIPTURE

"He was pierced for our transgressions, He was crushed for our iniquities; the punishment that brought us peace was on Him, and by His stripes we are healed" (**Isaiah 53:5, NIV**).

"'I will restore you to health and heal your wounds,' declares The Lord" (**Jeremiah 30:17, NIV**).

"As the rain and the snow come down from heaven, and do not return to it without watering the earth and making it bud and flourish, so that it yields seed for the sower and bread for the eater, so is my word that goes out from my mouth: It will not return to me empty, but will accomplish what I desire and achieve the purpose for which I sent it" (**Isaiah 55:10–11, NIV**).

REFLECTION

Grief can overwhelm your body, your nervous and immune system; every part of you. But God promises healing. Not just for your spirit and soul, but for your body too. Even when you feel too weak to move forward, He can breathe life and strength into you again. Ask Him to show you small ways to care for your body each day.

He is the Restorer. He is the Healer, and He will carry you through this. Speak life over your mind, body, soul, and spirit man, and just decree, declare, and believe. Healing and deliverance belong to the children of God. It is our inheritance.

His Word has power to restore and heal you. Decree and declare your healing and activate your faith. Healing is your inherited right. In the spirit realm, speak the Word and tell the enemy: You shall live and not die, and see the healing, deliverance, and manifestation of miracles of The Lord in the land of the living.

REFLECTION QUESTIONS

- How is grief impacting your body right now?
- What small steps can you take to begin releasing that physical pain?
- Who can you invite into your circle of support to walk this healing journey with you?

PRAYER

Father God, in the name of Jesus, this loss has touched not only my heart but my body. I feel weary, weak, and overwhelmed. But Your Word promises that by Your stripes, I am healed. You said you would restore my health and heal my wounds. So today, I receive Your healing power in my heart and in my body.

Strengthen me, Lord. Soothe my pain. Breathe new life into every part of me that feels broken or exhausted. Thank You for carrying me when I cannot carry myself. Thank You that You are healing my past, present, and future.

Thank You for healing my mind, not just over death, but my physical losses too. Jesus died so I can be redeemed. Thank You for restoring to me what the cankerworm and palmerworm came to destroy. You are restoring health to me and healing my wounds.

In Jesus' mighty name, Amen.

DAY 26
JOURNAL

They Already Know...

A lot of times in deep grief, after someone we love has died, we struggle with guilt. I know we've touched on guilt before, but just because someone says "don't feel guilty" doesn't mean it magically goes away. We wrestle with guilt a million times over, the should've, could've, and would've. The guilt we hold onto deserves time, space, and attention. One of the hardest things for many of us is the unfinished business.

"They left so suddenly. I didn't get a chance to..."

We replay moments, wondering if we could've done something different. We ask ourselves, "Did they know how I really felt? I should've called them. I should've visited. I never told them this. I wonder if they truly knew how much I loved them."

We carry those thoughts: I didn't show up enough. I didn't love them enough. I didn't do enough. Almost as if we should have known they were about to die and somehow we failed them.

I've been there. When my cousin passed, I had planned to call her. But that day, my body was exhausted from lupus, and I just wasn't up for talking. There were many days I thought to call, but I just wasn't up for it. By the time I reached out, she had passed unexpectedly. I carried that guilt for so long, wishing I'd just made that call.

When my grandmother passed, my last memory was

of her being frustrated because we kids jumped on her bed. That's how we left her house, and I never saw her again. When my Uncle Danny drove by one day, I didn't wave him down like I normally would. I knew he'd turn me around and send me home from where I was walking, so I let him pass. That was the last time I saw him.

There will always be moments we wish we could redo. There will always be a thousand "should haves." But here's the truth: You didn't know what you didn't know. I understand the guilt, the shame, and the regret you may feel, because I have felt them too. Your guilt may run deep. For that, I am so sorry. You are not alone. I have a thousand regrets. I sit with you in that space, sharing in some of those same regrets.

But one day, after therapy and after taking my regrets and sorrow to God in prayer, He encouraged me with these words: "I reconcile all things to Myself" (Colossians 1:20, NIV). That's why Jesus came and died, to free us from the burden of guilt, shame, and condemnation. So we wouldn't have to carry it, because He already carried it for us.

If you're struggling with guilt about whether your loved one knew how you felt, or wrestling with unfinished business, I pray these truths sweep over your heart. Even if you missed one last chance to talk, there were countless other moments when you hugged them, told them you loved them, and showed them care and affection. Your loved one carries those moments with them into heaven, not the unfinished or painful ones.

They know you loved them. They know you cared. They know your heart, and your desire to protect and cherish them.

Think about all the times you did protect them, guarded them, prayed for them, supported them, for as long as you've known them. In heaven, everything is reconciled. All misunderstandings and regrets are washed away. They don't carry pain or unfinished business. You didn't leave them.

Someone needs to hear that again: You. Didn't. Leave. Them!

God's love cancels every sin, every mistake, every human imperfection. When guilt whispers, listing all the things you could've or should've done, pause and write it down. Next to each lie, write the truth. Next to each accusation, write the reality of your love: I didn't get to call them, but I always called them.

We had so many calls filled with love. I never said I love you that one last time, but every time we spoke, I told them. I know they knew. I didn't protect them, but here's how I protected them throughout their life.

Write down each regret, and then write the truth beside it. Say to yourself: "This is the lie I'm hearing, but this is the truth I choose to stand on." Practice this. Speak truth until your heart finds peace. This may take time, because the enemy doesn't stop accusing. He stands before the Father day and night trying to condemn us.

But I'm here to tell you today: I'm proud of you. For the way you did show up. For the way you're working through your grief. For choosing to heal. Your loved one is proud of you too. They remember your kindness, your laughter, your care, even if your attempts were small or imperfect. Every act of love is remembered in heaven. They already know.

They know what you wish you could've said. They know what you wish you could've done, and from where they sit in heaven, they hold only your goodness, your love, and your light. They carry only the best of you. The Bible says in heaven, there are no more tears, no more sorrow, only peace.

I love you. I'm thinking of you, and I'm sending you the biggest hugs right now.

With love,
Ke'Shawn

SCRIPTURE

"For I will forgive their wickedness and will remember their sins no more." (**Hebrews 8:12, NIV**).

"He will wipe every tear from their eyes. There will be no more death or mourning or crying or pain..." (**Revelation 21:4, NIV**).

"If anyone builds on this foundation using gold, silver, costly stones, wood, hay or straw, their work will be shown for what it is... Only what is done for Christ will last" (**1 Corinthians 3:12–14, NIV, paraphrased**).

"Above all, love each other deeply, because love covers over a multitude of sins" (**1 Peter 4:8, NIV**).

REFLECTION

There is no sin in heaven. No pain. No score-keeping. No anger. No unfinished conversations. Your loved one isn't in heaven holding anything against you. They're not disappointed. They're not carrying resentment. You didn't let them down. They are healed. You are forgiven, and your hearts are forever reconciled. Heaven has already settled it all.

REFLECTION QUESTIONS

- What specific regrets or guilt do you feel about your loved one?
- If you could have told them one last thing, what would it be?

- What truth from God can you hold onto to help you release this guilt?

PRAYER

Father God, in the name of Jesus, I thank You for this day and the gift of life. I lift up the guilt I carry over what I did or didn't do for my loved one. Help me remember that I am only human, and I cannot change the past. Give me peace beyond understanding, knowing that everything is already settled in heaven.

Thank You for forgiving me, for freeing me from shame and condemnation. Because of Your blood, I am reconciled to You and reconciled with my loved one too. They know my heart. They know my intentions.

And now, I forgive myself and release this heavy burden into Your hands.

In Jesus' mighty name, Amen.

DAY 27
JOURNAL

_____

_____

_____

_____

_____

_____

_____

_____

_____

_____

_____

_____

_____

_____

_____

_____

_____

_____

_____

_____

_____

_____

_____

_____

_____

— DAY 28 —

Jesus!

The Bible says, "Hope deferred makes the heart sick" (Proverbs 13:12, NIV). In the midst of deep grief, especially with everything going on around us, the constant stream of losses, catastrophic news, and secondary losses can make our hearts feel sick. Right in the midst of grief, everything can feel dark and cloudy, like you're stuck in a forest and can't see any way out.

If you're in deep grief, I'm almost certain you'd ditto everything I'm saying and more. It is, indeed, the most horrible feeling in the world, and the pain doesn't let up. I'm here to acknowledge your pain and to sit with you while you're in the middle of this tumultuous storm. It would be my greatest hope that I could give you some Scripture that could make it better. Some kind of pain relief. Something I could say or do that would alleviate the agony in your soul, but the only remedy I have is Jesus.

He was a man of many sorrows, rejected, tortured, and experienced things we could never even imagine (Isaiah 53:3). Even the Son of God Himself cried out, "My God, My God, why have You forsaken Me?" (Matthew 27:46, NIV). Do you feel like God has forsaken you right now? Have you been suffering under this weight of grief for a while now, with no end in sight? It's easy to feel that way when someone we love dies—especially abruptly.

Where are You, God? Sometimes we can't hear Him. We can't feel Him. We can't see Him in the midst of the pain, and the suffering can feel like it will last forever. I pray that my story encourages you to just keep holding onto hope.

MY STORY

I've already shared how I felt about my grandfather, "Daddy." I've been blessed to have multiple fathers in my life, including my biological dad. My first family, the original crew, was my grandmother and grandfather, my sister, my uncles, and my mom. We were together day in and day out. We were all extremely close, a tight-knit family, with grandparents who were very hands-on.

I was my grandfather's baby, the baby of the family. But when my grandmother passed away, our matriarch and our angel, it was devastating. We were all in deep grief. My grandfather had to move. He was a truck driver, always on the road, so every time we were together, it felt like a family reunion.

Because he lived so far, I didn't get to see him often, and that was crushing. So many secondary losses came with my grandmother's passing. Fast-forward to my high school graduation, this was the moment he promised to take off from work, come home, and be there. We had big plans. Daddy was coming home.

Two days before graduation, my mom and I were getting ready to buy my graduation dress. There was excitement in the air. Just as I was heading out the door, my phone rang. I answered, and it was my grandfather's job calling.

I knew that call couldn't be good, and I was right. I was told he had passed away on the road.

Everything in me collapsed. There aren't words in the human language that could express the deep, dark despair that ripped my soul, 18 years old, two days before graduation. Graduation came and I showed up having an out-of-body experience. I was physically present, but my soul had checked out. I was numb and in a cloud.

I had worked so hard all those years in school, overcoming a misdiagnosis of a learning disability. I was in the top 10 percent of my class. I was an honor roll student, accepted into Iona University, which was not an easy school to get into, especially for someone who struggled with test-taking. I had awards and scholarships, and the day that was supposed to be a celebration of all I had come through came crashing down.

I didn't just lose a grandfather; I lost a father, Prince Cureton Sr. To this day, I can't remember anything about my graduation, and that deeply grieves me. I remember just sitting there, watching everything unfold around me, completely disconnected. There was no joy. There was no peace. Just agony and anger.

I spent that summer in a blur. I self-medicated. I made reckless decisions. I felt completely lost. My hopes and excitement for college and the future were just one big gray cloud.

I remember one night, coming home after being out for a while. My heart felt agonizing, unbearable pain. My body couldn't even contain it. My soul was in agony. I began to cry, and then my crying turned into travailing.

I collapsed on the floor in my street clothes at the foot of my bed. I cried and cried. I wailed, and then I cried out for Jesus. I begged Him, "Save me. Save me. Save me. Help me. Help me. Help me. Jesus! Jesus! Jesus! I can't take this pain! Help me!"

I can't tell you what happened next, because I collapsed. I passed out, and I have no recollection of what happened after that. It was like I blacked out. It felt like one of those big, steel animal traps with sharp claws had clamped down on my heart and soul, ripping me to shreds. I was beyond myself. I was eighteen years old and dying inside.

I woke up the next morning in my pajamas, under the covers, and that agonizing feeling was gone. There was peace in my room, and I knew Jesus had visited me in my despondency. I still can't tell you how I got in bed or how I got dressed in my PJs. I know that when I came home, my mom and my dad, Pete, were asleep. But I know this: for the first time in my life, I had an encounter with Jesus.

I cried out to Him, and He heard me. He delivered me from the agony in my soul. Did the grief disappear overnight? No. Did the pain and despondency vanish? Not exactly. But that torturous device gripping my heart was lifted off of me.

Only Jesus could do that, and it was the first time that Jesus became real to me. He was no longer just the man I was taught about in church with the picture on the wall. I had an encounter with Him, and He literally came in and delivered me from the agony of my soul.

So, wherever you sit today, I want to encourage you:

cry out to Jesus. Keep crying out to Jesus. Keep crying out to Jesus. "I cried to The Lord, and He heard me and delivered me from all my fears" (Psalm 34:4, NIV). "The cords of death entangled me; the anguish of the grave came over me… But in my distress I called to The Lord; I cried to my God for help. From His temple He heard my voice; my cry came before Him, into His ears" (Psalm 18:4–6, NIV).

God is no respecter of persons (Acts 10:34, NIV). If He came and rescued me, He will rescue you and keep rescuing you, even when grief feels like it's swallowing you whole. I sit with you in this moment. But more importantly, God sits with you. He sees you.

You are not forgotten. He understands your anger, your pain, your rage. Even the unforgiveness, toward Him or others. Whatever you're feeling today, you are seen. Hold on. Keep crying out.

I can't promise you when the storm will pass, or when the pain will lift. But the more you seek Him, the more you'll find Him. The more you call out, the more He will answer. The more you draw near, the more He will rescue you. One millisecond at a time, He will continue to rescue you over and over again.

Hold on and don't let go. Help is on the way. I love you and I'm thinking about you.

With love,
Ke'Shawn

SCRIPTURE

"The Lord said, 'I have indeed seen the misery of my people in Egypt. I have heard them crying out... and I am concerned about their suffering. So I have come down to rescue them...'" **(Exodus 3:7–8, NIV).**

"The Lord is close to the brokenhearted and saves those who are crushed in spirit" **(Psalm 34:18, NIV).**

"'I will restore you to health and heal your wounds,' declares The Lord" **(Jeremiah 30:17, NIV).**

REFLECTION

The Lord hears your cries. He's moved by your agony. He won't sit silently and allow you to drown. He will mount an angel and come down to sit with you, undergird you, and carry you. When He is silent, He is nearest; closer than the breath you breathe. Cry out to Him in your agony. It will echo in heaven, and all of heaven will come to your aid.

Your broken heart rings loudly, and all of heaven weeps with you. God is not far from the brokenhearted, but present and near, even if we don't feel Him. When you can't feel Him, or see His hand, seek His face. His character as Abba Father won't allow Him to ignore your state.

As a Father first, He will move the heavens to come to your aid. He proved it on the cross when He sacrificed His only Son so we can be reunited and not banished from His presence forever. Cry out to The Lord. He is right here, right now, with you in this moment.

REFLECTION QUESTIONS

- In what ways have you lost faith?
- What is the most agonizing part of your grieving process right now?
- How can you invite Jesus into this moment to help you?

PRAYER

Father God, in the name of Jesus, I come to You naked and bare, honest and raw. I'm not okay. I don't know when I'll ever be okay. I can't see the forest for the trees. There is no glimmer of joy or hope or the light of day. This grief, this loss, has ripped every form of joy I thought I could ever experience.

I know I have family and friends. I know there are things left to live for, but sometimes, I feel like I'm dying. Rescue me in the midst of my dying. Save my life, because I can't save myself. I'm being swallowed whole by the beast of this pain.

I give You my grief, my pain, my broken heart and my soul. I surrender it all to You. Take over, Lord. I can't do this anymore without You.

Ignite the embers and the fire of God in me. Ignite my faith, my hope, and my joy. Breathe life back into me. I feel dead, and everything around me feels like it's dying. I believe You are rescuing me. You are reviving me. You are healing me. You are delivering me. You are making me whole again, and I receive it.

In Jesus' mighty name, Amen.

DAY 28
JOURNAL

Precious Memories

o you ever find yourself thinking about a memory of your loved one and feel joy rip through the pain? These moments are a gift from God. In the midst of all our pain, there's nothing that brings us joy like the smile of our loved one, seeing their picture, hearing their voice, remembering a great moment, and reflecting on their love.

Many grieving people have shared that others, trying to be helpful, told them, "You've got to let the past go." Some even said professionals advised, "You need to move forward." While that may be true, no one can make you do it. Moving forward after loss takes time. Grief has many stages, and the journey doesn't follow a straight path.

You can be feeling multiple things at the same time. Grief can feel like a tangled web that's impossible to unravel. One moment you could be joyful, the next moment weeping, the next moment despondent. Sometimes you may be feeling all of the above.

For anyone telling you where you should be in your grief journey, please know this: you are your own grief expert. You are the authority on what you need, and your body, in its perfect wisdom, will do exactly what it's ready to do.

Depending on the type of loss you've experienced, early grief takes time to settle in. Early grief can still be the first few years of your grieving process, and sometimes longer. There is no timeline on grief. I deeply dislike when people try to rush others through this sacred process, especially when they say things like, "Don't dwell on the past. You need to move forward."

We've already discussed the model that Elisabeth Kübler-Ross introduced about the **stages of grief: denial, anger, bargaining, depression, acceptance, and finding meaning**. You will navigate these in your own time and your own way.

But I'm here to remind you of one of God's greatest gifts to us, no matter where you are in the process: memories. No one wants to be stuck in the past, but when our loved ones have transitioned, that's what we have left.

We have memories. We have the items they left behind. We have pictures. These are the things that keep us grounded in the midst of deep pain. They restore joy, they renew hope, and yes, sometimes they bring waves of sadness, but they are sacred reminders of the love that was shared.

They are reminders that they were on this earth, touched those items, and made those impacts. Who gets to tell you it's not okay to remember or reflect on the memories? The older we get, especially those of us experiencing our golden years, that's often all we have left. I'm telling you, that type of insensitivity makes me angry for people hurting so badly. Everybody grieves differently.

Some of us don't always have the time or space to fully sit with all of our emotions, but our feelings still matter. Our feelings still deserve to be honored. Whether we like them or not, they need to be felt. What we have to learn to do is create space for the love and the pain, to integrate both. Here's an exercise that I learned where you get to do both: feel the grief, and remember with love.

It's called the **30-Second Shift.**

STEPS

In the moments when you're deep in your grief, feel it. Experience it. Name it. Give yourself 30 seconds. Feel everything and allow the tears to flow.

NEXT:

After the 30 seconds are up, gently begin to shift your thoughts to a memory—to something that brings laughter, to something that brings comfort or joy. Even if your relationship wasn't everything you hoped for, consider what you learned in the process and what you're grateful for.

The most beautiful thing we get to take with us from our loved ones are the memories. So don't let anyone tell you to stop looking back. Don't let anyone shame you for remembering.

Remembering is a gift from God, and sometimes, in the beginning, the memories will hurt. But in the name of Jesus, millisecond by millisecond, over time, the pain will begin to shift. As David Kessler said, "You will begin to remember with more love than pain." So, give yourself permission to:

• cherish those memories

- Hold them tight
- Relish the pictures
- Play the songs
- Dance to the tunes
- Do the things they loved.

In the deepest pain, think about how you can honor them through the things they cherished, the passions they held, or the values they lived by. Here's the beauty. They get to live out their dreams in you now.

You get to merge the pain and the grief with finding the meaning in the pain. Carry their love and legacy with the world. YOU get to share them with the world and do things that will bring their life honor, even in their absence. That too is a gift. Whatever those things were, you get to carry them with you.

That is the greatest gift of all. So I sit here and re-member with you. I join you in relishing the beauty of all God has given you. Let those memories bring your heart comfort, even in the sorrow. But take your time, this too, is a process.

I love you, and I'm thinking about you.

With love,
Ke'Shawn

SCRIPTURE

"But the memory of the righteous is a blessing" (**Proverbs 10:7a, ESV**).

"I thank my God every time I remember you" (**Philippians 1:3, NIV**).

"Remember the former things of old; for I am God, and there is no other" (**Isaiah 46:9a, ESV**).

REFLECTION QUESTIONS

- In what ways can you honor your loved one by celebrating their life?
- What memory brings you the greatest joy?
- How can you use your memories as a gift to comfort you during times of grief?

PRAYER

Father God, in the name of Jesus, I'm grateful for today. I'm grateful for the gift of memories that flood my mind, sometimes leaving me in deep pain. I pray You give me pockets of time to remember, to laugh, to cry, to enjoy. Give me relief in being able to look back and remember.

You gave us the gift of memory so we would never forget, and so that it could help us hold onto hope as we move forward. Help me to create new things in my life, new ways to carry my loved one with me wherever I go. Help me to celebrate their life. I pray that every second of my life, You are leading me toward peace. Not a peace that says I'm okay with what happened, but a peace that allows me to live again with purpose, even with this sorrow.

Teach me how to bring my loved one into this new future on my journey with me. Give me grace and strength to hold it all together when I feel like I'm falling apart. Thank You for moments of joy, for Your divine winks throughout the day, for the reminder that You are near and that they live within me now. Remind me this is not goodbye, but "see you later." One day, we will be together again. Help me to be patient until that great reunion again and restore my joy again.

I thank You and love You, Lord.

In Jesus' mighty name, Amen.

DAY 29
JOURNAL

_____
_____
_____
_____
_____
_____
_____
_____
_____
_____
_____
_____
_____
_____
_____
_____
_____
_____
_____
_____
_____
_____

They Live On in Me

I spent 40 years of my life in deep grief. To the world, I was doing really well, successful in my career, doing all the right things on the outside. But what I didn't know was that the grief on the inside, and my inability to accept what was, was eating me up and killing me slowly.

As I've said before, it began to affect my body. I was in therapy one day, and the therapist said to me, "You're so busy looking at what you lost, you're not able to focus on the new, beautiful things God has brought into your life, your husband, your mom, your family, your kids. You're not able to really celebrate." For someone in early grief, you'd never say that. For someone who lost a child, someone really close to them, you'd never say that.

When you're deep in grief, you're not able to find the celebration. Forget celebration; how about finding breath and a glimmer of joy? My circumstance was a little different. For me, having been in grief for so long, for decades, I had never learned to shift. As we've talked about many times, grief takes time. But for me, I was never afforded the opportunity to grieve properly because of all my cumulative losses.

It had me stuck, where there was no **acceptance or finding meaning**. I had not allowed the healing process to begin. I had not allowed grief to transform me. I had no idea how to help myself in grief. I didn't know I wasn't helpless in its grip, that I had any power to help myself.

Grieving, and the process of finding meaning and acceptance, takes time, sometimes years, sometimes decades. I knew I was at a place where I wasn't able to move beyond where I was, and it had been decades. Growing up, therapy wasn't a thing like it is today. No one knew to go to therapy for grief.

I thought, and we all thought, that grief just gets better with time. Most people still think that. My family thought that too. When you're in insurmountable grief, it's all about trying to survive. They did the best they knew how with what they had. Looking back, I can see how much love and strength it took for them to keep going, even without the tools and resources we talk about more openly today.

Their faith, their resilience, and their care for me carried me through. But, at this stage of life, I know I was fully responsible for finding my healing. I felt the call of God to study, to learn, and to find my footing in this grief process in Him, and to refuse to let grief define me for even one day longer. The Lord and I began to look at Ecclesiastes: "To everything there is a season, and a time to every purpose under the heaven" (Ecclesiastes 3:1–4, KJV).

I also studied Revelation and 1 Thessalonians, where it talks about how we'll all be caught up in the air together, and that we do not grieve as the world grieves. "Brothers and sisters, we do not want you to be uninformed about those who sleep in death, so that you do not grieve like the rest of mankind, who have no hope" (1 Thessalonians 4:13, NIV).

Around the same time, my Aunt Patsy passed away. The funeral home called and told me they were going to bury her remains in our family plot, and I met them there.

She was my mentor, a woman I looked up to all my life, and someone I patterned myself after in my career. While they prepared her plot, I stood there and sobbed. I looked around and saw all my other family members buried there too. I felt the wave of grief that my entire family had all transitioned, all around me, and I mourned all of them. The scriptures I had been studying came to my mind in that moment.

Even though they brought comfort, I realized something important. Understanding scripture about death, grief, and loss brought so much comfort, but it didn't take the pain away. It didn't make it disappear. Knowing scripture alone didn't teach me how to grieve properly. It just masked the pain.

Now that I've been trained in grief education, I understand that my pain needed to be seen, processed, and sometimes even revisited. I needed comfort in ways I didn't even realize at the time.

At the cemetery, this was where scripture, faith, and my grief education met to process my pain. The Lord put in my heart at that moment what I needed to do. So as I stood in the cemetery, I looked all around me and allowed myself to feel everything.

Ecclesiastes came to mind. "To everything there is a season." I realized I had never had closure about what was. I had never paused in gratitude for what was gained, and as my mother would remind me about all of life's challenges, "In everything give thanks" (1 Thessalonians 5:18, NIV). I went to every plot of every person I had lost, on three hands I could count them, and I began to speak out loud, starting with my grandmother.

I allowed myself to cry, to feel, and to pray. I thanked her for the memories, the life she gave me, what she sowed into me, everything. I laughed and cried and let it all out. I celebrated her life, and for the first time, I released her.

I released her to her fate, and I declared mine. I will live, and not die, and see the miraculous salvation of The Lord. It took me decades to do that. I had been holding on to what was, and I was stuck. I had no idea I was stuck. I didn't even know I was grieving.

I didn't realize I was slowly collapsing and dying. With every death, a part of me had died too. But God was calling me to live, to let go of what I had lost. It was time. I spent the entire day at the cemetery.

I had never released any of them before. I thought that by letting them go, they would no longer exist, that their lives wouldn't matter. But God revealed to me that was the furthest thing from the truth.

Was I letting go of my love for them? No. Was I letting go of their memory? No. Was I letting go of what we shared? Absolutely not. Was I erasing their memory as if they never lived? NEVER. But I did need to decide that I was going to live.

Their fate was final on earth, and that was outside of my control. I realized that I wasn't living out my fullest life or potential because I had stayed in the grave with them. Grief had become unhealthy. It was no longer serving me. Outwardly, I appeared fine.

I wasn't mourning openly to others. But inwardly, my heart was truly sad that I lost my family. I never got over that. For every new thing God had given me, I relished it. But there was always a dark shadow that overcast it, so my joy never felt complete.

Grief was stealing the essence of my dreams, my joy, and robbing me of every single thing God was trying to give me. I couldn't shake what was. I was still grieving the family I had lost, my childhood family unit and our big family. I missed my family. All of them.

I couldn't move past that. But I was also missing the fullness of being in the now, the blessings right in front of me. The new family God had given me: my kids, my husband, new traditions, sisterhood, friends, a host of new mothers, fathers, new uncles and aunts, people who celebrated me. They weren't them, but God was making all things new. It didn't mean I had to let go of my original family, but I had to merge what was with what is.

So I sit with you today, not telling you to let your loved one go. I'll never say that. Here's what God shared with me, and I want to encourage you too: They may no longer be physically here, and His heart breaks, and my heart breaks with you because of that truth, and for that, I am so deeply sorry.

Here's one truth I never knew: Our love never dies! The gift God gave us is that they live on in us. We can take them wherever we go. They live on in us. We can find ways to bring them with us.

Our love gets to live on through time, space, and distance. This too is a gift from God. "He has made everything beautiful in its time" (Ecclesiastes 3:11, NIV). I know this wasn't the plan, and for that, I am so sorry. One day, I don't know when or how, but I believe by faith (and I'm holding that faith for you) that God will plant that same revelation in your heart. He will breathe life into the places within you that have grown weary, awaken what has died, and transform your deepest pain into something beautiful in its time.

It will take time, and that's okay. This part of the journey takes prayer and a whole lot of time. In Jesus' name, I decree and declare He will guide you here too, in its time.

What I've learned through death is that sometimes death overshadows life. We get so bogged down with grief, and rightfully so, but often, we lose sight of the life.

This too takes time. What I've come to learn is that their lives are not just their deaths. They lived. They laughed. They gave us memories.

Their love, care, spirit, and soul touched our lives and left their fingerprints on the earth. We owe it to them to celebrate that life. Their legacy absolutely gets to live on in you. Does this happen overnight? Absolutely not.

I will never sit here and minimize your loss and say this part of the journey is easy. I know, without even knowing, it has taken your breath away. It took me decades. But one millisecond at a time, if we allow God, He can do the shift as we put our hand in His, and we trust Him with the process.

So ask yourself right now:

- What can I do to remember them?
- How can I honor them?

- What part of them gets to live on through me?
- How can I show the world who they were?

Right now, I also want to thank you. Thank you for entrusting me with this part of your journey.

Thank you for investing in this book, investing in your self-care and healing, and more importantly investing in the possibility of what God can do with your pain.

He desires you to know, in your deepest pain: **"healing is still possible and available to you!"** Despite your worst nightmare, you can still be healed and whole, in Jesus' name! So, as He has instructed me to speak over you,

"Be Healed and Whole in Jesus' name!"

I'm proud of you, and more importantly, God is proud. It took courage to go through this 30-day journey of healing.

I congratulate you for coming this far, and I thank you for allowing me to walk with you through these 30 days. It has always been my daily prayer for God to heal the land. I pray that every pain I've endured, every tear I've cried, every loss I've endured would not only heal me, but birth healing in others. I'll never get my loved ones back, and there's nothing that can happen that could undo that. Full redemption is not just God healing me, but helping others to heal with me.

I pray, somehow, my pain can help in someone else's process and bring new life and new light. With our broken heart in one hand, and our other hand holding onto The Lord, we can rise again and fulfill our call and purpose.

That's true redemption, and it breaks the back of the enemy.

Beloved, The Lord wants you to know that you are seen. You matter. Your grief, pain, healing, and loved one matters, and you are not alone. How you feel and what you've been through matters. God desires you to draw closer to Him.

He desires to heal every facet of your pain. He wants to make all things new. He will never dismiss the fact that you have just been through the most devastating loss of your life. You're hurting, and your life is no longer the same. That matters to God in Christ Jesus.

He also wants you to know their death doesn't define them, your love for them does, and they live on in you. It's not what you would have ever imagined, your worst nightmare.

Jesus Christ, the Almighty, the powerful One who controls everything, who gives strength to the weary and power to the weak, can resurrect you right now, where you sit, where you feel dead on the inside. He can give you the ability to rise again. I know you don't see it. I know you don't understand how it could ever happen again, but if God raised Jesus from the dead, He can shift and do a miracle in you.

Your loved one gets to live, not in the way you would like it or the way you ever imagined, but they get to live on in you. I believe God on your behalf. I hold faith and strength for you, and I declare, in the name of Jesus, that He will resurrect what has been lost, what has been stolen, and breathe new life into you right now and every day, until you close your eyes.

So, the journey continues, one millisecond at a time, one second at a time, one moment at a time. The Lord will not let go of you. He is with you. Shalom, the peace of God, the love of God in Christ Jesus, envelop you right now, and everything concerning you. Before we close out today, I want to decree and declare a blessing over you. This blessing is rooted in scripture, but also drawn from the song "The Blessing" by Cody Carnes and Kari Jobe. May it bless your soul too.

"The Lord bless you and keep you; The Lord make His face shine upon you and be gracious to you; The Lord lift up His countenance upon you and give you peace" (Numbers 6:24–26, NKJV).

"May His favor be upon you and a thousand generations, for your family and your children, and their children, and their children's children" (Deuteronomy 7:9; Exodus 20:6, NIV).

"May His presence go before you, and behind you, and beside you, all around you, and within you. He is with you" (Exodus 33:14; Psalm 139:5, NIV).

"In the morning, in the evening, in your coming and your going, in your weeping and rejoicing, He is for you" (Deuteronomy 28:6; Psalm 30:5, NIV).

You too, can pray this prayer over yourself and your family. I love you. Thank you for allowing me to join you on this journey.

I'm praying for you, and I'm thinking about you.

With love,
Ke'Shawn

SCRIPTURE

"I will not leave you as orphans; I will come to you" (**John 14:18, NIV**).

"...to bestow on them a crown of beauty instead of ashes, the oil of joy instead of mourning, and a garment of praise instead of a spirit of despair" (**Isaiah 61:3, NIV**).

"I will restore to you the years that the locust has eaten" (**Joel 2:25, NIV**).

REFLECTION

We didn't imagine our life this way. But this is our reality. So the question is: **What will you do with the pain you feel?**

That's the question God asked me. It's the question He asks you now. I had allowed grief to define me. Christ Jesus came that you shall live and not die and see His salvation.

Death and grief came, and that changed your existence. But He desires you choose to live again, to give Him space and time to make you whole again.

Where your faith is broken, He wants to renew it again. All He asks is your surrender. He desires to fix the broken pieces. One act of faith. He'll meet you right where you are. He wants to remind you He loves you with an endless love. All He asks is for you to come, so you both can heal, together.

REFLECTION QUESTIONS

- How can you take your pain and turn it into purpose?
- In what ways can you honor your loved one's life?
- What areas are you struggling to let go of?
- How can you support your healing by releasing the things sabotaging it?
- Where can you find a circle of support to help you heal?
- What small step can you take today to remember with more love than pain?

PRAYER

Father God, in the name of Jesus, I thank You for today. I thank You for this devotional. I ask that You bless the writer, and I pray that You bless me. I pray in the name of Jesus that every day of my life, You help me define my grief and turn my pain into purpose. I know it doesn't happen overnight, but You are the God of miracles, and I can expect transformation, healing, and newness every day.

Thank You for the grace that sustains me. Thank You for this devotional that I can return to, reread, and allow to continue to heal me. Help me find sparkles of joy in my sorrow. Give me the capacity to feel and process my pain in healthy ways.

Steal my joy back. Heal my body. Heal my soul. Resurrect what's dead in me and breathe life into my dry bones. I receive Your healing. I receive resurrection power, and I thank You for reviving me again and again and again, and restoring the joy and gladness in the midst of my pain.

Thank You that You will never leave me or forsake me, and I don't have to do this alone.

Thank You for walking with me through it all. I am not alone. Jesus Christ, the Son of God, is with me. You will never let me go. I shall live and not die and decree and declare the salvation, the miracles, signs and wonders in the miraculous of The Lord in the land of the living.

In Jesus' mighty name, Amen.

Day 30
Journal

Bonus Features

Prayers

WHY IS IT IMPORTANT TO PRAY?

Prayer is crucial in our walk with God. It's our connection and lifeline to Him. Prayer also breaks the back of the enemy. When you pray and believe, it moves heaven to act on your behalf. When you speak God's Word out loud, you not only weaken the forces of darkness and bind its power, but you also release God's power to shift, change, transform, empower, and heal. Prayer calls heaven to earth.

Especially when you pray scripture, like the ones included below, you are declaring God's Word, His legal document in the spirit realm, and His Word will do what it says.

Does that mean every prayer gets answered the way we want? Not always. But when we pray in faith, we are speaking those things that are not as though they are, and God honors that faith (Romans 4:17, NIV).

Our role is not to force His hand but to activate our faith through prayer. Prayer releases angels to carry out God's assignments on our behalf (Psalm 103:20, NIV).

If you pray, things can shift in heaven and on earth. If you don't pray, nothing moves. My mother used to tell me as a child: "Your prayers have the power to save someone's life." Your prayers have power! Simple prayers, like a child's, can move a mountain (Matthew 17:20, NIV).

Prayers can break Generational Curses and cycles of

suffering passed down from previous generations. Through prayer, we invite God's power to heal what has been broken, restore what was lost, and create new patterns of freedom, peace, and blessing for generations to come.

Ultimately, the decision rests with God. His will prevails, but He calls us to exercise our faith, even faith the size of a mustard seed, and trust Him with the outcome. You can pray these word-for-word, or use them as a guide to lift your own prayer to God.

If you have never accepted Jesus Christ as your Lord and Savior, here's your opportunity to do so now. If your trials have shaken your faith and you want to give your life back to The Lord, this is your chance to start fresh and recommit yourself to Him.

PRAYER OF SALVATION, COMMITMENT, AND SURRENDER

Father God, in the name of Jesus, we thank You for this day. We thank You for the gift of life.

I come humbly before Your throne, broken and shattered. But Your Word says You are close to the brokenhearted (Psalm 34:18, NIV), and You bind up our wounds (Psalm 147:3, NIV). You said if we draw near to You, You will draw near to us (James 4:8, NIV).

Your Word also says that if we believe in The Lord Jesus and the finished works of the cross, that He died for our sins, forgives our sins, rose from the grave, sits at the right hand of God the Father and will come back with our loved ones to receive us if we confess with our mouth and believe with our heart that Jesus Christ is the Son of God and Savior of the world, we shall be saved (Romans 10:9–10, NIV).

So Father, I recommit myself to You right now. I surrender my life, my will, my emotions, my family, my future, my legacy, my assignment, my purpose, everything for which You created me, I surrender to You now.

I turn over complete control to You. I ask that You come into my heart, come into my life, and make me over again. I can't change what happened. I'm a broken vessel. You are the potter; I am the clay (Isaiah 64:8, NIV).

I ask You to rescue me and change me from the inside out. That I will live and not die, and see the salvation of The Lord (Psalm 118:17, NKJV).

I commit to You right now. In the name of Jesus, block the hands of the enemy from killing, stealing, and destroying (John 10:10, NIV).

Cover my family under the blood of Jesus. Father, forgive us all for our sins. Wash our bloodline with the blood of Jesus, making us clean again. Cover us under Your blood. Cancel every generational curse, familiar spirit, and ancestral curse over my family line, cancel them right now in the name of Jesus.

Thank You for the Son of God, Jesus Christ, who brings new life and resurrection power into me and my family.

Thank You for Your sacrifice on the cross and for receiving me right now. Thank You for shutting the door to every legal right the enemy had in my life.

The old has passed away, behold, You are doing a new thing (2 Corinthians 5:17, NIV).

I receive the baptism of the Holy Spirit right now, in the name of Jesus. Fall fresh.

Let the breath of God breathe new life into me right now (Ezekiel 37:5, NIV).

I breathe in and receive Your Spirit.

I breathe out every demonic thing that has ever tried to kill, steal, or destroy me.

I receive You, Lord Jesus, right now, and I thank You for the victory.

In Jesus' mighty name, Amen.

PRAYER TO STRENGTHEN AND GROW YOUR WALK WITH CHRIST DAILY

Father God, I thank You for my life and for loving me. I ask You, the glorious Father of our Lord Jesus Christ, to give me spiritual wisdom and understanding so I can grow in knowing You more.

Open the eyes of my heart and flood me with Your light so that I can clearly see the hope You have given me and the wonderful future You have promised for me and my family. Help me to understand how rich and amazing this inheritance is for those who belong to You.

I pray that I will also begin to understand how great Your power is for those of us who believe in You. This is the same mighty power that raised Jesus Christ from the dead and seated Him at Your right hand in heaven (Ephesians 1:16–20, NLT).

Lord, when I think about how wide Your plan is and how much wisdom is in it, I can only bow before You in prayer. You are the Creator of everything in heaven and on earth.

I pray that out of Your glorious and endless riches, You would give me strength in my inner being through the Holy Spirit. I pray that Jesus will feel at home in my heart as I trust in Him more and more. May my roots grow down deep into the soil of Your love.

I ask that You help me grasp, along with all of Your people, just how wide, how long, how high, and how deep the love of Christ really is. I want to experience His love, even though it is so big that I will never fully understand it.

Fill me with the fullness of life, and the power that only comes from You.

Now to You, God, be all the glory! By Your mighty power working in me, You are able to do far more than I could ever dare to ask, dream, or imagine. May You receive all glory in the church and in Christ Jesus throughout every generation, forever and ever. Amen (Ephesians 3:14–21, NLT).

In Jesus mighty name, Amen!

Grief Education Glossary

Acceptance – A stage of grief where you begin to acknowledge the reality of your loss. Acceptance doesn't mean forgetting or "moving on." It means learning to live again while carrying your loved one with you. (Day 4, 13, 18, 24, 29, 30)

Anticipatory Grief – Grief experienced before a loss happens, such as when a loved one is terminally ill, aging, or declining. (Day 6)

Belief Systems – What your faith says about life, death, and what comes after. It can bring immense comfort, peace, and calm to the storm you may be facing. (Day 6)

The Body Keeps Score – The reality that grief and trauma live in the body, often showing up as inflammation, illness, aches, or other physical symptoms when unprocessed. (Day 26, Reference)

Complicated Grief – When grief remains prolonged, intense, and disruptive, making it difficult to function in daily life. (Grief Education Glossary)

Collective Grief – Shared grief experienced by a group, community, or nation, such as after tragedies, disasters, or widespread loss. (Grief Education Glossary)

Cumulative Loss – Multiple losses over time (death,

divorce, health, finances, relationships) that stack and intensify grief. (Introduction, Day 11, 14, 30)

Disenfranchised Grief – Grief that isn't always recognized or validated by others—like miscarriage, suicide, loss of a pet, or estranged relationships. (Day 13)

Elisabeth Kübler-Ross's Five Stages of Grief – A well-known model describing common grief experiences (not linear, people may move back and forth): (Day 4, 29)

- **Denial** – "This can't be happening." Shock, numbness, or disbelief
- **Anger** – Rage or frustration toward God, self, or others.
- **Bargaining** – "If only…" thoughts or trying to change the outcome.
- **Depression** – Deep sadness, withdrawal, hopelessness.
- **Acceptance** – Recognizing the reality of the loss and learning to live again.

Faith and Grief – Trusting God in the midst of loss. Faith doesn't erase grief, but it gives strength, peace, and hope for the future. (All Days – especially 28 & 30, Grief Education Glossary)

Fears in Grief – Common fears include: forgetting your loved one, grieving too long, breaking down in public, feeling like the pain will never end, or fearing the future. These fears are normal and deserve compassion. (Day 14)

Fight-or-Flight – A physiological response that occurs

when your body stays on high alert, preparing to protect you from real or perceived danger. (Day 14)

Fight / Flight / Freeze / Fawn – The body's survival responses when it feels unsafe or overwhelmed: (Day 9, Day 14, Day 19)
- **Fight** – Anger, lashing out, trying to control grief.
- **Flight** – Avoiding grief, staying busy, or running from emotions.
- **Freeze** – Feeling numb, stuck, or unable to move forward.
- **Fawn** – People-pleasing or over-caretaking to avoid conflict or pain.

Finding Meaning: Recognizing that even in loss, life has purpose, and there may be lessons, growth, or new understanding that come from your grief. (Day 30)

Generational Curses – Patterns of trauma, sin, or brokenness passed down in families. Believers can pray for freedom and break these cycles through Christ. (Day 30, Prayer)

Grief – The natural, human response to loss. It includes emotional, physical, spiritual, and mental reactions. (All Days)

Grief Bursts – Sudden waves of grief that come without warning, often triggered by a memory, anniversary, smell, or sound. These remind us that grief is not linear. (Day 13, 22)

Grief Brain – Mental fog, forgetfulness, and cognitive overwhelm during grief, caused by stress on the nervous system. It makes decision-making and memory difficult. (Day 19, 21)

Grief Coach – A trained guide and companion who walks alongside individuals in grief, offering tools, strategies, and compassionate support to help them navigate loss. (Day 21, 26)

Grief Education – Learning what grief is, how it works, and how to support yourself and others. Builds grief literacy and breaks myths about grief. (Grief Education Glossary)

Grief Group Support – A safe space (often in churches, communities, or organizations) where people gather to share grief experiences, receive encouragement, and find community healing. (Grief Resources, Day 26, Grief Education Glossary)

Grief Literacy – Understanding what grief is, how it affects your mind, body, and spirit, and learning how to talk about it with care and compassion. (Day 20)

Grief Illiteracy – The lack of understanding or skills to respond to grief with empathy and care. (Day 20)

Grief Movement Guide – A trained facilitator who helps grievers process their emotions through safe physical movement, body-based practices, and breath work. (Day 26)

Grief Peer-to-Peer Support – Informal support where people who've been through grief share experiences with others currently grieving. It provides connection and reduces isolation. (Grief Resources, Day 26, Grief Education Glossary)

Grief Work – Being intentional about processing your grief, gaining coping and resiliency tools, and working through your emotions. It means actively doing something with the pain in a healthy way so you can recover and move through it instead of getting stuck in it. (Day 21)

Grief Triggers – Things that bring grief to the surface (holidays, birthdays, places, songs). Triggers are normal and part of ongoing grief. (Day 25)

Inner Critic – The harsh inner voice that shames, blames, or condemns. Spiritually, this reflects the "accuser" in scripture (Revelation 12:10). (Day 22)

Legacy – The love, memories, and values someone leaves behind that live on through you. (Introduction)

Loss – Not just death, but any kind of separation or absence: divorce, health decline, miscarriage, financial loss, home, friendships, or identity. (All Days, Day 22)

Neuroception – The body's subconscious way of scanning the environment for safety or danger, often heightened during grief. It influences nervous system reactions. (Day 19)

New Normal – Life after loss won't return to how it was. This phrase describes adjusting to a permanently changed reality. (Day 22)

Old Wounds – Past grief or trauma that resurfaces when new losses occur. Sometimes unhealed pain from childhood, family dysfunction, or earlier losses influences how we grieve today. (Day 6, 25)

Parasympathetic Nervous System (PNS) – The "rest and restore" system of the body. It calms stress, lowers heart rate, aids digestion, and helps healing. Activated through prayer, stillness, breathing, and safety. (Day 14, 26)

Resiliency Tools – Practical supports for healing, such as journaling, scripture meditation, prayer, counseling, community, and healthy movement. (Day 21)

Secondary Losses – Losses connected to the primary loss (losing a spouse also means losing companionship, income, or shared dreams). (Day 18)

Stuck Grief – When grief does not move forward or soften over a prolonged period of time, often because emotions are unacknowledged or suppressed. It is also known as complicated grief or chronic grief. (Grief Education Glossary)

Sympathetic Nervous System (SNS) – The body's "fight, flight, freeze, or fawn" stress response. It heightens alertness and prepares for danger but, when stuck in overdrive, can cause anxiety, insomnia, or body pain. (Day 14)

Task Mode – A grief coping state where you avoid emotions by focusing on tasks: planning, cleaning, organizing, or helping others. It feels productive but often masks deeper pain. (Day 8, 21)

Trauma – A wound to the body, mind, or soul caused by overwhelming events like sudden death, violence, tragedy, or abuse. Trauma complicates grief and often requires additional support. (Day 6)

Triggers in the Body – Grief affects the body with symptoms like migraines, chest pain, stomach upset, fatigue, or immune system issues. (Day 6, Day 25, Day 28)

Types of Grief – (Grief Education Glossary, Day 6, Day 8, Day 30)
- **Normal Grief** – Sadness that gradually softens over time.
- **Anticipatory Grief** – Grief before the loss happens.
- **Complicated Grief** – Intense grief that disrupts life long-term.
- **Disenfranchised Grief** – Grief not socially recognized.

- **Collective Grief** – Shared grief after community tragedies or events.

Validation of Grief – Affirming that your grief is real and important, no matter what others say. (Grief Education Glossary)

Wheel of Emotions – A tool by psychologist Robert Plutchik showing how emotions connect and overlap. It helps grievers name complex feelings like sadness, anger, fear, joy, or surprise. (Day 3)

David Kessler's Six Needs of the Grieving – A framework describing what grieving people truly need (Day 25, Grief Education Glossary):

1. To have your pain witnessed – Someone to listen without judgment or fixing.
2. To express your feelings – Permission to feel and release emotions.
3. To release the burden of guilt – Freedom from self-blame.
4. To be free of old wounds – Healing past hurts that grief brings up.
5. To integrate the loss – Finding ways to carry your loved one forward.
6. To find meaning – Discovering purpose in life after loss.

Grief Resources

Disclaimer: This book is for education and encouragement only. I am not a medical professional. If you are in crisis or contemplating self-harm, please call **988** in the U.S. for the Suicide & Crisis Lifeline, or **911** for immediate emergency assistance.

National & International Grief Resources
- **Grief.com** – Resources, articles, and programs from grief expert David Kessler.
- **Tender Hearts Grief Support Community (David Kessler)** – A private online community offering connection and support: www.grief.com
- **Grief Recovery Institute** – Evidence-based programs for individuals and organizations: www.griefrecoverymethod.com
- **Compassionate Friends** – Support for families after the death of a child: www.compassionatefriends.org
- **Dougy Center** – Grief support for children, teens, young adults, and families: www.dougy.org
- **GriefShare** – Christ-centered grief support groups held in churches worldwide: www.griefshare.org
- **Good Grief (New Jersey)** – Grief support and education for children, teens, and families: www.goodgrief.org

TRAINING PROGRAMS

- **Grief Educator Certification Program (David Kessler)** – Professional training to deepen grief literacy and provide grief-informed care: www.grief.com
- **Paul Denniston's Grief Movement Training** – Movement-based healing for grief: https://www.pauldennistontraining.com/grief-movement-training
- **Alex Howard's RESET Program** – Nervous-system -based healing tools for trauma, stress, and chronic illness: www.alexhoward.com
- **Dora Carpenter's Grief to Gratitude Coaching Certification** – Professional grief coach training and certification: www.fromgrieftogratitude.com

CRISIS RESOURCES

- **988 Suicide & Crisis Lifeline** – Call or text **988** (U.S. only).
- **911** – If you are in immediate danger or medical crisis.

For international crisis hotlines: see findahelpline.com.

SERVICES BY KE'SHAWN HILL-ADAMSON

UnStuck Worldwide LLC

Certified Grief Coach | Grief Educator | Grief Movement Guide | Grief & Loss Public Speaker | Fellow Courageous Griever

The mission of UnStuck Worldwide is to be a guiding light, illuminating the darkness of grief. Our vision is for the brokenhearted to heal and recover—transitioning from grief, loss, and pain to discover meaning, joy, and purpose.

About Me

As a Certified Grief Educator, Coach, Grief Movement Guide, and Public Speaker, I provide tailored grief education and support to individuals and organizations. Trained by grief expert David Kessler and Emmy-nominated public speaking coach Rachel Hanfling, I specialize in:

- Grief, loss, & pain public speaking
- Grief education & group support
- Grief training & consulting for businesses, churches, and organizations
- Resiliency strategies & workshops
- Grief movement & meditation (safe, chair-based, body -centered practice)

With lived experience of grief, health challenges, and resilience, my mission is to be the help I once needed— walking with others to transform pain into purpose.

Booking Information

Website: www.unstuckworldwide.com
Email: unstuckworldwide@gmail.com
Social Media: **@unstuck_worldwide** (all platforms)

Celebrating Life

&

Legacy!

My Dad "Pete"

My Dad "Pete" & Daddy

We love you, and you will be missed!

Uncle David

"Daddy"

Grandparents & Great Grandparents

"Mommy"

Great Grandma Nana, Grandpa, "Mommy,"
& Great-Grandma Fannie

Grandma Johnnie

Grandpa Dudley

Grandpa Ollie

Great Grandpa Daniel

Great Grandpa Mr. Hill

Here my handprints are done
for everyone to view
I had so much fun
Doing this for you.

So look upon this handprint plaque
Hanging on your wall
And memories will come back
of me when I was small

Prince

Lil Cuz
Prince Shaquan Cureton III

"Daddy"

HOMEMAKING PROVES REWARDING IN SUBURBS
Entertaining, Social and Civic Duties Make Life Full

Betti Logan

Gloria Brown has had the best of two worlds—business and homemaking. For 20 years she was an accounting supervisor in the audit division of the Internal Revenue Service. Now she is the wife of one of Black Enterprise's Top 100 Businessmen, mother of a grown daughter and a homemaker.

Trading in a business career for apron strings and lots of free time has not been a problem for her. The adjustment was easy—in fact, she prefers the new life. "Although I enjoyed my job very much, I like staying home much more," she says. "When I was coming along, black women generally had to work to supplement a husband's income. Today, however, things are different. Work is more a luxury than a necessity for many women. Now women are looking for fulfillment in a job as well as a good salary.

Her husband, Daniel, part owner of VIP Lincoln-Mercury dealership in New Rochelle, N.Y., often comes home to lunch with Gloria. His Main Street office is just 15 minutes away from the Brown's five-room Cape-style house. "Although I love our dates, I'm not always home. Dan and I have an understanding. I follow my own plans," she explains.

Gloria was not always this independent. There was a time in her life when she was unable to make plans. "Before I knew Dan I was shy, quiet and withdrawn. But when we met—it was life at first sight," she says, remembering back to that summer at Cape Cod.

"Dan is the kind of person who will bring anyone out of their shell, and that's exactly what he did for me," she says smiling. "Dan loves people. He could be with them 24 hours a day."

Entertaining is one of the Brown's favorite pastimes, and something they do quite often. "Sometimes we have a race to see who can come up with the most reasons for giving a party," she says.

Midday is Gloria's favorite time to entertain friends and a champagne brunch is the way she likes to do it.

Most of the Brown's entertaining is done in their wood paneled basement because the dining area upstairs is too small.

BLACK ENTERPRISE / JANUARY 1975

Uncle Danny

Uncle Danny

St. Catherine A.M.E. Zion Church

New Rochelle
Settled at least by the Huguenots from La Rochelle

Uncle Danny & Aunt Gloria

Cousin Tommy, Uncle Danny, Aunt Gloria, Uncle Clifford

Cousin Tommy, Uncle Danny, Auntie, Uncle Clifford, Uncle Jack, Grandma Fannie

My Family

Cousin Kedrick

PLANES
Mustang Pilots Take
Part in Raid On
German Capital

Three Jet Planes

Uncle Jac

Uncle Clifford
& Aunt Ora

Drew Hill

Dudley And

Uncle Drew

Aunt Patsy

Uncle Ri

Cousin Kedrick

Aunt Mel

Cousin Laverne

My Family

"Grandma" Abrahams

Uncle Howard

Andre

Andre

Mr. Taylor

Ma Bunny

My Dad, "Pete"

Uncle Ray

Mrs. Brown

Uncle Larry, Grandma,
Great-Grandma Dora

Uncle Joe

Brother Olandis

References

Scripture Translations

The Holy Bible: English Standard Version. Wheaton, IL: Crossway, 2001. (All Days, Day 29)
The Holy Bible: King James Version. Cambridge: Cambridge University Press, 1769. (All Days, Day 30)
The Holy Bible: New International Version. Grand Rapids, MI: Zondervan, 2011. (All Days, especially Day 28 and Day 30)
The Holy Bible: New King James Version. Nashville, TN: Thomas Nelson, 1982. (All Days, Day 30)
The Holy Bible: New Living Translation. Carol Stream, IL: Tyndale House, 2015. (All Days, Day 22, Day 29)

Books

Denniston, Paul. *Healing Through Movement: The Grief Movement Guidebook. New York: HarperOne, 2023. (Day 26)*
Kessler, David. *Finding Meaning: The Sixth Stage of Grief. New York: Scribner, 2019. (Day 29, Day 30)*
Kübler-Ross, Elisabeth. *On Death and Dying. New York: Macmillan, 1969. (Day 29)*
Kübler-Ross, Elisabeth, and David Kessler. *On Grief and Grieving: Finding the Meaning of Grief Through the Five Stages of Loss. New York: Scribner, 2005. (Day 29, Day 30)*
Plutchik, Robert. *Emotion: A Psychoevolutionary Synthesis. New York: Harper & Row, 1980. (Glossary –*

Wheel of Emotions, Day 3)
van der Kolk, Bessel. *The Body Keeps the Score: Brain, Mind, and Body in the Healing of Trauma. New York: Viking, 2014. (Day 26)*

Articles

Medical News Today. "How Grief Affects the Body: Physical Symptoms and Health Risks." *Medical News Today, 2023. (Day 26, Glossary) UCLA Health. "The Connection Between Grief and the Body." UCLA Health, 2024. (Day 26, Glossary)*

Programs and Training

Carpenter, Dora. *Grief to Gratitude ICF-Accredited Grief Coaching Program. Institute of Professional Grief Coaching. (Glossary)*
Denniston, Paul. *Grief Movement Training. Grief Movement Method. (Day 26)*
Howard, Alex. *The Reset Program: Healing Trauma and the Nervous System. Alex Howard and Conscious Life, 2022. (Day 19, Day 26; Glossary)*
Kessler, David. *Grief Educator Certification Program. Grief.com. (Day 26, Day 30)*

Support & Resources

GriefShare. *Support Groups for Grief Recovery. Church Initiative, 2024. (Day 30; Glossary)*
Compassionate Friends. *Support for Families After a Child Dies. 2024. (Day 30; Glossary)*
National Alliance for Children's Grief. *Support and*

Education Resources. 2024. (Day 30; Glossary)

Music
Carnes, Cody, and Kari Jobe. *The Blessing. Elevation Worship, Capitol CMG, 2020. (Day 30)*

Key Terms & Concepts
Porges, Stephen W. *Polyvagal Theory: Neurophysiological Foundations of Emotions, Attachment, Communication, and Self-Regulation. New York: W.W. Norton, 2011. (Day 19; Glossary – Nervous System)*

Trauma and nervous system terms (fight, flight, freeze, fawn, neuroception) adapted from trauma-informed psychology literature. (Day 19; Glossary)

Social Media & Online Content
@goodneuroscience (Instagram). Content on the neurobiology of crying and grieving. (Day 12)

Notes for Publisher/Reader

Statistics and Medical Facts — Information cited from *Medical News Today (2023) and UCLA Health (2024).*

Book and Glossary Sources — This book and glossary draw from grief-education frameworks taught by David Kessler, Elisabeth Kübler-Ross, Paul Denniston, Alex Howard, Dora Carpenter, and other trauma-informed grief educators and trainings. Their teachings have informed and shaped my understanding of grief, which I have expressed here in my words, reflections, and devotional practice. Any concepts that may reflect or resemble their teachings are included with full acknowledgment of their influence on my training and practice.

Scripture Quotations — All scripture quotations are taken from the Bible translations listed in the reference section.

About Ke'Shawn Hill-Adamson

$\mathcal{K}$e'Shawn Hill-Adamson is an accomplished Certified Grief Educator, Coach, Grief Movement Guide, Writer, Author, Blogger, and Public Speaker. She is certified by the International Coaching Federation–accredited Institute of Professional Grief Coaching as a Certified Grief Coach. Ke'Shawn is being mentored and has been certified by world-renowned grief expert David Kessler, becoming a Certified Grief Educator and trained Co-Moderator for specific losses in his Tender Hearts group grief support program. Additionally, she is a Certified Grief Movement Guide under Paul Denniston, helping individuals process grief that is stuck in their bodies through movement, breath, and sound. Moreover, she is certified in Mental Health First Aid.

Ke'Shawn has also trained under Rachel Hanfling, an Emmy-nominated TV Producer (*The Oprah Winfrey Show and Anderson Cooper*), Media and Communications Trainer, and International Keynote Speaker—in her Own the Power of Your Story training in Public Speaking for Grief Educators. She specializes in coaching, grief group facilitation, public speaking, and workplace training on grief and loss.

She holds a Bachelor's Degree in Mass Communications

with a specialization in Advertising and a Master of Arts and Science Degree (Summa Cum Laude) in Corporate Communication, specializing in Program Development and Design, from Iona University. She also holds a certification in Women's Entrepreneurship from Cornell University. Moreover, she is an alumna of the NASDAQ Entrepreneurial Center Milestone Circles for Women Entrepreneurs and a member of ForbesBLK.

Throughout her career, which has included roles in advertising, academia, and program development and management, Ke'Shawn's personal journey with grief and her experience overcoming health challenges, including morbid obesity and lupus, have deeply transformed her life. This lived experience enables her to provide the kind of support she once needed, guiding others in rebuilding and healing after devastating loss.

As Founder and CEO of UnStuck Worldwide LLC, Ke'Shawn empowers and equips individuals, businesses, and organizations with customized grief education, support, and resilience strategies. Her work focuses on being a guiding light, illuminating the darkness of grief. Her vision is for the brokenhearted to heal and recover, transitioning from grief, loss, and pain to discovering meaning, joy, and purpose.

Ke'Shawn is a contributing author of multiple works that center healing, connection, and purpose, including *Dads Deserve It Too: Honoring the Love of Fathers, What Makes You Smile?: Joy | Happiness | Gratitude, and a peer-reviewed publication in Growing Through Grief.* All titles are available on Amazon. She also founded B.O.O.M.! (Break, Obliterate & Overcome Mountains!), a faith-based blog inspiring resilience and purpose at boom4christ.com.

Married for 16 years with two beautiful daughters, Ke'Shawn cherishes her many roles as a wife, daughter, sister, best friend, and founder of a ministry. She embraces her journey from leadership in the workforce to stay-at-home motherhood and is now emerging as a passionate mompreneur. Her faith is her cornerstone, providing strength, guidance, purpose, and resilience through life's toughest challenges.

For more information, visit:

www.unstuckworldwide.com.

Acknowledgments

To my Father, **James D. Gates**, Thank you for every sacrifice you've made, every lesson taught, every memory and time well spent. Thank you for showing up when I needed you the most and making and creating so many memories with me and our family.

I'm so grateful He allowed us another opportunity to be in each other's lives, that truly was a gift of God. Thank you for allowing me to stretch and pull you in ways to grow our relationship.

Thank you for every memory you've made with me and for always being a part of my life's major transitions. You are a giant of a man to me, my inspiration. Thank you for being a rock and passing on such a rich legacy of what resilience, success, and determination look like, and for pouring into your grandbaby Lizzie, your grandmother's namesake.

Thank you for everything. I love you, Daddy.

To my husband, **Richard Adamson II,** One of the greatest men that has walked the planet. You have changed my world. You are what agape love looks like. A heart of gold, a manly man, that holds down his family, that goes hard day and night.

You took all kinds of abuse in the workforce to take care of your family, always putting us first. Your sacrifices weren't in vain. No matter what, you come in that door with a smile, loving on each of us. You are my forever and always, the love of my life, the one that makes my heart sing, that still gives me butterflies, my best friend, my covering, my biggest advocate, my earthly hero and protector who holds me down in ways that's unexplainable. Thank you, my baby.

You've been my rock during life's toughest transitions, from losing my dad, to major losses in our family, and the difficulties I faced after having Elizabeth in my health. Thank you for doing it with such grace and love, compassion, and care.

Thank you for all the ways you spoil and dote over me. You have always loved the little girl in me, and now, you love the adult too, helping both to heal. You have watched me evolve, and God put me in your heart from when we were pre-teens. Thank you for never stopping pursuing me from the time we were teenagers. Me and you, forever and ever. I'd fight devils and demons covering you, it's me, you, and Jesus against the world.

I luv you, my king!

To my girls, **Cydnei & Elizabeth**, Every day I wake up, I go hard because I'm thinking of you. Every day, I'm slaying giants, forging paths, and speaking life over you, leaving behind a lasting legacy and breaking generational curses so you can forge your own path and break barriers of your own in following Christ.

You are great women of God, valiant warriors, who hold the power of the keys of heaven and hell in your hand. Only what you do for Christ will last. Thank you for believing in me, supporting me on my journey, and showing up when I need it. I love you with my everything!

To my parents-in-love, **Pastor Richard & First Lady Carol Adamson**, Thank you for pouring into me and our family. Thank you for all the wisdom, time spent, and investment, the prayers of covering and unconditional love.

I love you and thank you for loving me as your very own. Thank you for believing in me, praying me through all my processes and rooting me on. You truly showed me love and kindness.

I love and am so grateful and couldn't have asked for better parents-in-love, ever.

Honoring the late **Bishop Brown and First Lady Sarah Brown**, First Lady Sarah Brown, God sent you into my life to transition me from a growing young adult, to a valiant soldier in Christ and stellar professional.

Under your leadership, you not only understood the spiritual war I was in at work when on assignment in the workforce, but you taught me how to slay giants that come against me, how to love people when sometimes they're unlovable, how to be wise as a serpent and innocent as a dove.

Thank you for seeing my worth, my smarts, and for speaking life into me when the days got hard at work. Every chance you met with me you spoke life into me. And when I was struggling the most, you continued to speak life and sat with me for hours, training me to be who I was becoming.

You always told me God was doing a quick work in me, that I had a tremendous amount of responsibility at a very fast and young age, and you've watched me rise to the occasion. Your fingerprint will forever be on my life, not only as a woman of God, but in every business endeavor that I do. Thank you for believing in me and helping me spread my wings and fly.

Thank you to the Brown family for your love and support over the years and also for being a part of our adopted family.

To **Pastors Clarence and Tresmaine Grimes**, There are no words to express our gratitude for all the seeds you have sown into my life and into my family's life. You are our spiritual parents, but also our second parents.

Dr. Tresmaine Grimes, we first met at Iona University at a retreat. Out of all the doctors there, you were the one that stood out and was different. Your kindness and compassion spoke to me just in a small encounter.

You were the one God used to pray, be my buffer, and help rout demons off of my life. God chose you and Pastor Clarence to lay down our marital foundation as our marital counselors.

You both counseled us for years in the midst of me losing my Dad Pete, which rocked our foundation, and supported me after many other losses with other family, when the breath was taken out of me. We often would sit, we'd talk, and God used you to help breathe the breath of God back into me.

For every different phase of my life when the enemy was trying to take me out, you positioned yourself to be a buffer and sowed into me and my family.

You may not have birthed us, but the spiritual connection God has given supersedes any natural occurrence of birth. You are Mommy and Dad Grimes.

Thank you for every financial seed, every form of support, for being our spiritual counselors, everything. I can go on and on and on about our relationship. There are no words that can ever express our gratitude. Thank you both for being our secondary parents and helping Richard and me set the foundation for almost 17 years of marriage now. We love you and we thank you.

To **Toishishuma, Tia, Gisel, and Nicole**: my best friends: Thank you for seeing me, believing in me, being my biggest cheerleader and praying me through, and loving me unconditionally when I wasn't at my best.

Thank you for decades of memories, laughs, and walking me through life transitions into adulthood. We have decades of memories to last a lifetime. You have been my ride-or-dies, my listening ears, my support. No matter what the need is, you jump in like a storm to help fix it. I've lost so much family, and God sent each of you to fill in those voids along with your families.

To the **Abrahams family, Michelle Hayes, the Slater family, the Surpris family, the Taylor family,** my Godsons **Ijani** and **Izziah**, and the **Tirado and Feliciano family**, you welcomed me into your family as your own. Thank you for loving me like family. My deepest love and gratitude to you all.

Each of you has added to and changed my life, and I'm so grateful God sent you to me.

To my sister circle: **Dr. Leah Johnson and family, Rochelle Salmon McKenzie and family, Sheila Harris, Aesha Sharrieff & family, Lu & Tracy Humphreys, Euralis Figueroa, Ashley Gooden-Stewart, Demetress Harrell, Rev. Yasmin Harris, and Melissa Santiago,** thank you for your love, support, planting seeds in me, and guidance over the years.

To my Church Families:

Thank you to my first church family, **St. Catherine A.M.E. Zion Church (former pastor Dr. Michael J. Rouse, current pastor Pastor Wallace Noble & congregation**).

To my home church, **Gospel Tabernacle Church of Christ (Pastor Richard Adamson Sr. and First Lady Carol Adamson, to all of the elders, Elder Wellington, Elder Jesse Prince, my husband Elder Richard Adamson II**, and the Gospel Tabernacle family).

To my extended church family, **Living Water Christian Center** (Pastors Clarence and Tresmaine Grimes & congregation).

To **Abundant Love Apostolic Church (Pastor Ricardo & First Lady Roxanne Smalls, Founders Bishop & First Lady Brown** & congregation).

Thank you for what you have sowed into my life. Eternal thank-yous!

To my **extended family: Adamson, Patterson,**

Wilson-Whynn, Cureton, Gates, O'Faire, Brown, Mitchell, Hill, Redd, Montague, Evans, White, Beaman, Horitano, Washington, Payne, Carrington Arms family, all my sisters, brothers, nieces, nephews, aunts, uncles, cousins, I love you and thank you for your love and support.

Honorable Mentions & Special Thank-Yous

To **David Kessler** and the **Grief.com** team, **Krista Richards**, and my **Grief Educators alumni circle**: David, thank you for every conversation, every seed you've sown, and for dedicating your life to helping others not just heal, but recover after devastating loss. Your work has not only helped heal me, but it has transformed my life. I am a better me, a more whole and healed me, because of you. Your fingerprints and teachings are all over this work. Thank you for helping give me my wings to fly. You have truly helped change my life and given me the courage to walk more confidently and boldly into my calling in this sacred space of serving others in grief. To my fellow Grief Educators, I am eternally grateful to each of you and the role you've played in my life.

To **Paul Denniston**, Founder of Grief Yoga & Grief Movement Training: Without even knowing it, during our class time together, I was extremely sick. I was later diagnosed with Lupus. Your compassion and your work gave me the voice to express the heart-wrenching pain I was feeling not only in my body, but in my soul. Thank you for giving me tools to process the grief and pain I was carrying in those moments when I was silently crying out. It truly transformed how I coped with the loss of my health. It allowed me to pray through movement and cry out in my devastation. What you offer is a gift that was birthed in pain. Thank you for sharing it with the world. God sent you at that exact time to help me. I am eternally grateful.

To the **Grief to Gratitude Program and Founder Dora Carpenter:**
Thank you for your loving-kindness and for giving me my first foundation. Thank you for sowing generously into me and helping me to find my calling. I found it!

To **Rachel Hanfling,** Emmy-Nominated Media & Public Speaking Coach: Your fingerprint will be on every speech and talk I do. Thank you.

To **Kate Bialo**, Founder of Furniture Sharehouse. To the **NASDAQ Entrepreneurial Center, Milestone Circles.**
To SCORE of Westchester County.
To SCORE Business Mentor, **Peter Diamond**.
To SCORE Web Expert, **Anne Kasdin**.
To **Michael Tedesco**.
To **Audre Hauser**.

To **True Vine Publishing**. I am eternally grateful for each of you; for every seed you've sown, every sacrifice you've made, the love you've given, the prayers you've prayed, and the time you've invested in believing in me to bring me to where I am today.

For anyone I didn't name, I'm truly sorry. Please charge it to my head and not my heart. Eternally grateful to each and every one of you.

With love,
Ke'Shawn Hill-Adamson

ORDER MORE COPIES:
www.Unstuckworldwide.com

Retail Price: $29.99 per book
Shipping $6.00 (Add $1 for each additional book)

Order with cash or check

Buyer Name: _____

Mailing Address: _____

_____

Qty_____ x $29.99
Shipping; $6 for the first book + $1 per additional book.

Subtotal: $_____

Shipping $ _____

Total: $_____